D1530243

Know Him

Know
Him

A YEAR OF DAILY BIBLE READINGS
ON THE CHARACTER OF GOD

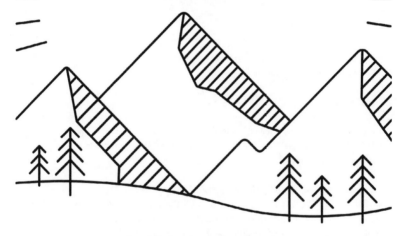

Joel Armstrong
General Editor

Our Daily Bread
Publishing.

Know Him: A Year of Daily Bible Readings on the Character of God
© 2023 by Our Daily Bread Publishing

Interior design by Darren Welch

ISBN: 978-1-64070-218-9

Printed in China
24 25 26 27 28 29 30 31 / 9 8 7 6 5 4 3 2

CONTENTS

Getting to Know God

From beginning to end, the Bible is God's story to us, revealing who He is through His actions, words, and relationships.

"In the beginning God created the heavens and the earth" (Genesis 1:1). From the first page of His story, we already see that God is creative, sovereign over heaven and earth, and unimaginably powerful as He calls into being massive stars and tiny fish with a few words.

"Then I saw 'a new heaven and a new earth,' for the first heaven and the first earth had passed away. . . . He who was seated on the throne said, 'I am making everything new!'" (Revelation 21:1, 5). And at the end, God is still showing himself to be the same person He's always been: the true King of the world, faithful to His people and promises, who has never stopped creating things anew.

Today, there are many things we hope to find in the Bible's pages. Maybe we're looking for spiritual self-improvement, because our minister said we should read it. Or relief, because we feel guilty that we're not. Maybe we want that feeling of approval we get when we tell a friend what we read in God's Word this morning.

Our reasons for reading Scripture are often based on what we've been told the Bible *is*. A road map for getting through life. A moral compass to guide our decision-making. An instruction booklet for all our spiritual questions.

It's worth asking, How did Jesus, God himself incarnated as a human being, approach Scripture? At the beginning of His ministry, Jesus read from the prophecies of Isaiah about miraculous healings, freedom for the oppressed, and good news for the poor. "Today this scripture is fulfilled in your hearing," Jesus said (Luke 4:21). The Scriptures pointed to Jesus, to His just character and His work of redemption. And after He rose from the dead, Jesus appeared to two of His disciples who were struggling to understand His sudden, brutal death on a cross. To make sense of His death and resurrection, Jesus again turned to the Bible. "Beginning with Moses and all the Prophets, he explained to them what was said in all the Scriptures concerning himself" (24:27). He looked to Scripture to reveal a Person.

Whatever our previous expectations of the Bible, this time let's look for it to speak to us about who God is. Throughout Scripture's pages, we'll find a complex, profound, and sometimes overwhelming portrait of God. He is love. He is utterly holy. He is here and everywhere at once. He is three in one. He is righteous and just and merciful and faithful and all-knowing. He became human but is infinite, far beyond our comprehension, incapable of being fully expressed through written books (John 21:25).

Yet we long to know this person who created us, loves us, and redeems us. Even if words like *everlasting* and *holy* can't contain Him, they are tools He himself has given us to understand Him. So, in this year of daily readings, each month we will look at one of God's attributes revealed in the Bible: His glory, transcendence, truth, and so much more. And every day, we'll look at passages from the Psalms, from the Old Testament, and from the New Testament to deepen our understanding.

In preparing to explore God's character in this devotional, I immediately wondered, Where should we start? With the apostle John's most famous declaration, "God is love" (1 John 4:8)? With the first words of creation, when God discloses himself as the source of all our own creativity? There are many excellent starting points. However, as I began to map God's attributes onto each month, I considered how the seasons of our Christian calendar highlight different aspects of His character: During Christmas, we savor God's love, His immanent desire to be "God with us" (Matthew 1:23). During Lent, in the days leading up to Easter, we remember God's mercy, that He is slow to anger and compassionate with our sins. During Epiphany we see God's wisdom in bringing salvation to all nations, and in celebrating the transfiguration we see God's unveiled glory. Whether it is part of your church tradition to observe Advent, or Pentecost, or the ascension, these moments from New Testament history point us to distinct facets of God's person, and so the readings here do that as well.

And yet *not* distinct facets of God's person! There are differences, of course, between God's love and His holiness. But in studying His love we will see His relationality, and we cannot even talk about His holiness without describing how He is wholly other from all beings He is in relationship with. So as we spend this year surveying God's character, we will return to familiar aspects of who He is and experience the rich overlap between His traits of *faithfulness* or *justice* or *mercy*, because God is not contradictory, and all of His attributes fit together into a perfect whole.

Each set of readings is short, easily digestible in a few minutes. But I pray these passages linger with you throughout your day, and that as you accumulate them throughout these weeks and months, a fuller picture of our great God will take shape for you from the pages of Scripture. May you "grow in the grace and knowledge of our Lord and Savior Jesus Christ. To him be glory both now and forever! Amen" (2 Peter 3:18).

—**JOEL ARMSTRONG,** general editor

Wise

O boundless Wisdom, God most high,

O Maker of the earth and sky,

who bid'st the parted waters flow

in heaven above, on earth below.

The streams on earth, the clouds in heaven,
by thee their ordered bounds were given,
lest 'neath the untempered fires of day
the parchèd soil should waste away.

E'en so on us who seek thy face
pour forth the waters of thy grace;
renew the fount of life within,
and quench the wasting fires of sin.

Let faith discern the eternal Light
beyond the darkness of the night,
and through the mists of falsehood see
the path of truth revealed by thee.

O Father, that we ask be done,
through Jesus Christ, thine only Son;
who, with the Holy Ghost and thee,
doth live and reign eternally.

Author unknown, 6th century
translated from Latin by Gabriel Gillett

The Wisdom of God's Creation

PSALM 104:24–25

How many are your works, LORD!
In wisdom you made them all;
the earth is full of your creatures.
There is the sea, vast and spacious,
teeming with creatures beyond number—
living things both large and small.

JEREMIAH 10:12–13

But God made the earth by his power;
he founded the world by his wisdom
and stretched out the heavens by his understanding.
When he thunders, the waters in the heavens roar;
he makes clouds rise from the ends of the earth.
He sends lightning with the rain
and brings out the wind from his storehouses.

ROMANS 11:33–36

Oh, the depth of the riches of the wisdom and knowledge of God!
How unsearchable his judgments,
and his paths beyond tracing out!
"Who has known the mind of the Lord?
Or who has been his counselor?"
"Who has ever given to God,
that God should repay them?"
For from him and through him and for him are all things.

What is one thing God has created that demonstrates His wisdom to you? Pray and thank Him for His unsearchable understanding.

The Wisdom of God's Works

PSALM 111:7–8, 10

The works of his hands are faithful and just;
    all his precepts are trustworthy.
They are established for ever and ever. . . .

The fear of the LORD is the beginning of wisdom;
    all who follow his precepts have good understanding.

JOB 28:26–28

When he made a decree for the rain
    and a path for the thunderstorm,
then he looked at wisdom and appraised it;
    he confirmed it and tested it.
And he said to the human race,
    "The fear of the Lord—that is wisdom,
    and to shun evil is understanding."

1 CORINTHIANS 2:7, 9–10

We declare God's wisdom, a mystery that has been hidden and
that God destined for our glory before time began. . . . As it is written:

"What no eye has seen,
    what no ear has heard,
and what no human mind has conceived"—
    the things God has prepared for those who love him—

these are the things God has revealed to us by his Spirit.

~

*Lord, thank you for revealing your wisdom through your great
works and glorious purposes. Teach me the fear of the Lord—awe
and reverence for you.*

The Wisdom of God's Ways

PSALM 19:7–8

> The law of the LORD is perfect,
>   refreshing the soul.
> The statutes of the LORD are trustworthy,
>   making wise the simple.
> The precepts of the LORD are right,
>   giving joy to the heart.
> The commands of the LORD are radiant,
>   giving light to the eyes.

PROVERBS 3:5–7

> Trust in the LORD with all your heart
>   and lean not on your own understanding;
> in all your ways submit to him,
>   and he will make your paths straight.

> Do not be wise in your own eyes;
>   fear the LORD and shun evil.

JAMES 3:17–18

The wisdom that comes from heaven is first of all pure; then peace-loving, considerate, submissive, full of mercy and good fruit, impartial and sincere. Peacemakers who sow in peace reap a harvest of righteousness.

~~~~

God's wisdom is pure, peace-loving, considerate, merciful, fruitful, impartial, and sincere.

God's Wisdom and the World's "Wisdom"

PSALM 49:3, 5–6

My mouth will speak words of wisdom;
    the meditation of my heart will give you understanding. . . .

Why should I fear when evil days come,
    when wicked deceivers surround me—
those who trust in their wealth
    and boast of their great riches?

JOB 12:13, 17, 21

To God belong wisdom and power;
    counsel and understanding are his. . . .
He leads rulers away stripped
    and makes fools of judges. . . .
He pours contempt on nobles
    and disarms the mighty.

1 CORINTHIANS 1:21–23, 30

For since in the wisdom of God the world through its wisdom did not know him, God was pleased through the foolishness of what was preached to save those who believe. Jews demand signs and Greeks look for wisdom, but we preach Christ crucified. . . . It is because of him that you are in Christ Jesus, who has become for us wisdom from God.

In what area of your life are you trusting the world's wisdom rather than God's? Talk with Him about it, asking Him to open your eyes to His ways.

God's Wisdom and Our Sin

PSALM 51:3, 5–6

For I know my transgressions,
> and my sin is always before me. . . .
Surely I was sinful at birth,
> sinful from the time my mother conceived me.
Yet you desired faithfulness even in the womb;
> you taught me wisdom in that secret place.

JOB 9:2–4

But how can mere mortals prove their innocence before God?
Though they wished to dispute with him,
> they could not answer him one time out of a thousand.
His wisdom is profound, his power is vast.
> Who has resisted him and come out unscathed?

JAMES 3:14–16

But if you harbor bitter envy and selfish ambition in your hearts, do not boast about it or deny the truth. Such "wisdom" does not come down from heaven but is earthly, unspiritual, demonic. For where you have envy and selfish ambition, there you find disorder and every evil practice.

~~~~

Lord, I know the places in my heart where I struggle with envy, bitterness, and selfish ambition. Please teach me your wisdom instead.

The Invitation of God's Wisdom

PSALM 90:10, 12

Our days may come to seventy years,
or eighty, if our strength endures. . . .
Teach us to number our days,
that we may gain a heart of wisdom.

PROVERBS 1:20, 22–23

Out in the open wisdom calls aloud,
she raises her voice in the public square. . . .
"How long will you who are simple love your simple ways? . . .
Repent at my rebuke!
Then I will pour out my thoughts to you,
I will make known to you my teachings."

EPHESIANS 3:10–12

His intent was that now, through the church, the manifold wisdom of God should be made known to the rulers and authorities in the heavenly realms, according to his eternal purpose that he accomplished in Christ Jesus our Lord. In him and through faith in him we may approach God with freedom and confidence.

God wants to share His wisdom freely with you.

Jesus, the Fulfillment of All Wisdom

PSALM 49:13–14

> This is the fate of those who trust in themselves,
>> and of their followers, who approve their saying.
> They are like sheep and are destined to die;
>> death will be their shepherd
>> (but the upright will prevail over them in the morning).
> Their forms will decay in the grave,
>> Far from their princely mansions.

ISAIAH 11:1–2

> A shoot will come up from the stump of Jesse;
>> from his roots a Branch will bear fruit.
> The Spirit of the LORD will rest on him—
>> the Spirit of wisdom and of understanding,
>> the Spirit of counsel and of might,
>> the Spirit of the knowledge and fear of the LORD.

COLOSSIANS 2:2–3

> My goal is that they may be encouraged in heart and united in love, so that they may have the full riches of complete understanding, in order that they may know the mystery of God, namely, Christ, in whom are hidden all the treasures of wisdom and knowledge.

What word or phrase from the passages above stood out to you?
Pause to talk with God about it.

God Knows Every Word

PSALM 139:4–6

Before a word is on my tongue
you, Lord, know it completely.
You hem me in behind and before,
and you lay your hand upon me.
Such knowledge is too wonderful for me,
too lofty for me to attain.

ISAIAH 40:27–28

Why do you say, Israel,
"My way is hidden from the Lord;
my cause is disregarded by my God"?
Do you not know?
Have you not heard?
The Lord is the everlasting God,
the Creator of the ends of the earth.
He will not grow tired or weary,
and his understanding no one can fathom.

MATTHEW 6:7–8

When you pray, do not keep on babbling like pagans, for they think they will be heard because of their many words. Do not be like them, for your Father knows what you need before you ask him.

~~~~~

Lord, thank you that you already know every word hidden in my heart. I want to rest in the knowledge that you are behind and before me, with your loving hand upon me.

God Knows Every Heart

PSALM 44:20–21

> If we had forgotten the name of our God
>   or spread out our hands to a foreign god,
> would not God have discovered it,
>   since he knows the secrets of the heart?

JEREMIAH 20:11–12

> But the LORD is with me like a mighty warrior;
>   so my persecutors will stumble and not prevail.
> They will fail and be thoroughly disgraced;
>   their dishonor will never be forgotten.
> LORD Almighty, you who examine the righteous
>   and probe the heart and mind,
> let me see your vengeance on them,
>   for to you I have committed my cause.

REVELATION 2:23

> All the churches will know that I am he who searches hearts
> and minds.

God knows every thought in every person's mind, and every desire in every person's heart.

God Knows Every Secret

PSALM 90:8

> You have set our iniquities before you,
>   our secret sins in the light of your presence.

DEUTERONOMY 29:29

The secret things belong to the LORD our God, but the things revealed belong to us and to our children forever, that we may follow all the words of this law.

MATTHEW 6:5–6

And when you pray, do not be like the hypocrites, for they love to pray standing in the synagogues and on the street corners to be seen by others. Truly I tell you, they have received their reward in full. But when you pray, go into your room, close the door and pray to your Father, who is unseen. Then your Father, who sees what is done in secret, will reward you.

~~~~~

Is there something you're doing publicly that's really just between you and God? Or something you're hiding that you need to disclose to someone safe? Talk with God about it. He already knows.

God Knows All Time

PSALM 147:4–5

He determines the number of the stars
    and calls them each by name.
Great is our Lord and mighty in power;
    his understanding has no limit.

PROVERBS 8:22–26

The LORD brought me forth as the first of his works,
    before his deeds of old;
I was formed long ages ago,
    at the very beginning, when the world came to be.
When there were no watery depths, I was given birth,
    when there were no springs overflowing with water;
before the mountains were settled in place,
    before the hills, I was given birth,
before he made the world or its fields
    or any of the dust of the earth.

HEBREWS 4:13

Nothing in all creation is hidden from God's sight. Everything is uncovered and laid bare before the eyes of him to whom we must give account.

~~~~

Lord, you know everything in my past, everything in my present, and everything in my future. Please help me to rest in your limitless wisdom.

God Knows the Unknowable

PSALM 139:16–18

> All the days ordained for me were written in your book
> before one of them came to be.
> How precious to me are your thoughts, God!
> How vast is the sum of them!
> Were I to count them,
> they would outnumber the grains of sand.

ISAIAH 40:13–14

> Who can fathom the Spirit of the LORD,
> or instruct the LORD as his counselor?
> Whom did the LORD consult to enlighten him,
> and who taught him the right way?
> Who was it that taught him knowledge,
> or showed him the path of understanding?

1 CORINTHIANS 2:10–11

The Spirit searches all things, even the deep things of God. For who knows a person's thoughts except their own spirit within them? In the same way no one knows the thoughts of God except the Spirit of God.

God knows every hidden thing, including every unknown that worries you.

God Knows Us Completely

PSALM 139:1–3

> You have searched me, LORD,
>   and you know me.
> You know when I sit and when I rise;
>   you perceive my thoughts from afar.
> You discern my going out and my lying down;
>   you are familiar with all my ways.

1 KINGS 8:38–40

When a prayer or plea is made by anyone among your people Israel . . . then hear from heaven, your dwelling place. Forgive and act; deal with everyone according to all they do, since you know their hearts (for you alone know every human heart), so that they will fear you all the time they live in the land you gave our ancestors.

ACTS 1:24–25

Then they prayed, "Lord, you know everyone's heart. Show us which of these two you have chosen to take over this apostolic ministry, which Judas left to go where he belongs."

How does it comfort you to know that God knows everything you are and everything you do? Share what you're feeling with Him, and ask Him to teach you to see yourself the way He sees you.

God's All-Knowing Discipline

PSALM 94:11–12

> The LORD knows all human plans;
> he knows that they are futile.
>
> Blessed is the one you discipline, LORD,
> the one you teach from your law.

PROVERBS 2:6

> The LORD gives wisdom;
> from his mouth come knowledge and understanding.

JOHN 21:17–18

> The third time he said to him, "Simon son of John, do you love me?"
> Peter was hurt because Jesus asked him the third time, "Do you love me?" He said, "Lord, you know all things; you know that I love you."
> Jesus said, "Feed my sheep. Very truly I tell you, when you were younger you dressed yourself and went where you wanted; but when you are old you will stretch out your hands, and someone else will dress you and lead you where you do not want to go."

~~~~~~

Lord, I'm so grateful that you want to share your wisdom with me. Please show me where I need your understanding, guidance, or discipline in my life.

God Is Everywhere

PSALM 139:7–10

> Where can I go from your Spirit?
>> Where can I flee from your presence?
> If I go up to the heavens, you are there;
>> if I make my bed in the depths, you are there.
> If I rise on the wings of the dawn,
>> if I settle on the far side of the sea,
> even there your hand will guide me,
>> your right hand will hold me fast.

PROVERBS 5:21

> For your ways are in full view of the LORD,
>> and he examines all your paths.

ACTS 17:24

The God who made the world and everything in it is the Lord of heaven and earth and does not live in temples built by human hands.

~~~

God is present everywhere, from the heavens to the depths.

God Sees Everything

PSALM 33:13–15

From heaven the LORD looks down
and sees all mankind;
from his dwelling place he watches
all who live on earth—
he who forms the hearts of all,
who considers everything they do.

PROVERBS 15:3

The eyes of the LORD are everywhere,
keeping watch on the wicked and the good.

MATTHEW 10:29–31

Are not two sparrows sold for a penny? Yet not one of them will fall to the ground outside your Father's care. And even the very hairs of your head are all numbered. So don't be afraid; you are worth more than many sparrows.

Where in your life do you feel like God isn't seeing you? Pray to Him, thanking Him that He sees every sparrow that falls, knows every hair on your head, and cares deeply for you.

God Is Near Everyone

PSALM 14:2

> The LORD looks down from heaven
>   on all mankind
> to see if there are any who understand,
>   any who seek God.

JEREMIAH 23:23–24

> "Am I only a God nearby,"
> declares the LORD,
>   "and not a God far away?
> Who can hide in secret places
>   so that I cannot see them?"
> declares the LORD.
>   "Do not I fill heaven and earth?"
> declares the LORD.

ACTS 17:26–27

From one man he made all the nations, that they should inhabit the whole earth; and he marked out their appointed times in history and the boundaries of their lands. God did this so that they would seek him and perhaps reach out for him and find him, though he is not far from any one of us.

~~~~~

Lord, thank you that you are near my friends and loved ones, everyone I know and everyone I pass on the street. Please help the people in my life to become more aware of your presence with them.

God Sees in Light and in Darkness

PSALM 139:11–12

> If I say, "Surely the darkness will hide me
>> and the light become night around me,"
> even the darkness will not be dark to you;
>> the night will shine like the day,
>> for darkness is as light to you.

JOB 34:21–23

> His eyes are on the ways of mortals;
>> he sees their every step.
> There is no deep shadow, no utter darkness,
>> where evildoers can hide.
> God has no need to examine people further,
>> that they should come before him for judgment.

JOHN 1:3–5

Through him all things were made; without him nothing was made that has been made. In him was life, and that life was the light of all mankind. The light shines in the darkness, and the darkness has not overcome it.

There is no darkness in your life or in the world that God cannot see and overcome.

God Sees Every Decision

PSALM 10:11–14

He says to himself, "God will never notice;
   he covers his face and never sees."

Arise, Lord! Lift up your hand, O God.
   Do not forget the helpless.
Why does the wicked man revile God?
   Why does he say to himself,
   "He won't call me to account"?
But you, God, see the trouble of the afflicted;
   you consider their grief and take it in hand.

JEREMIAH 17:10

I the Lord search the heart
   and examine the mind,
to reward each person according to their conduct,
   according to what their deeds deserve.

COLOSSIANS 1:16–17

For in him all things were created: things in heaven and on earth,
visible and invisible, whether thrones or powers or rulers or authorities;
all things have been created through him and for him. He is before all
things, and in him all things hold together.

~~~

*What is one choice in your life that you're grateful God oversaw?
Thank Him for knowing every choice you've made and how those
choices affect your relationships with those around you.*

God Is Near His People

PSALM 11:4

> The LORD is in his holy temple;
>> the LORD is on his heavenly throne.
> He observes everyone on earth;
>> his eyes examine them.

ISAIAH 43:2

> When you pass through the waters,
>> I will be with you;
> and when you pass through the rivers,
>> they will not sweep over you.
> When you walk through the fire,
>> you will not be burned;
>> the flames will not set you ablaze.

MATTHEW 18:18–20

Truly I tell you, whatever you bind on earth will be bound in heaven, and whatever you loose on earth will be loosed in heaven.

Again, truly I tell you that if two of you on earth agree about anything they ask for, it will be done for them by my Father in heaven. For where two or three gather in my name, there am I with them.

~~~~~~

Lord, so many times your other followers have pointed me to your presence and wisdom. Thank you for the community of believers you've put in my life.

God Goes with Us

PSALM 32:8

I will instruct you and teach you in the way you should go;
I will counsel you with my loving eye on you.

DEUTERONOMY 31:6

Be strong and courageous. Do not be afraid or terrified because of them, for the LORD your God goes with you; he will never leave you nor forsake you.

JOHN 10:2–4

The one who enters by the gate is the shepherd of the sheep. The gatekeeper opens the gate for him, and the sheep listen to his voice. He calls his own sheep by name and leads them out. When he has brought out all his own, he goes on ahead of them, and his sheep follow him because they know his voice.

~~~

God always goes with you, even in places that are unfamiliar or daunting.

The Wisdom of God's Will

PSALM 135:5–7

I know that the LORD is great,
    that our Lord is greater than all gods.
The LORD does whatever pleases him,
    in the heavens and on the earth,
    in the seas and all their depths.
He makes clouds rise from the ends of the earth;
    he sends lightning with the rain
    and brings out the wind from his storehouses.

1 SAMUEL 2:6–8

The LORD brings death and makes alive;
    he brings down to the grave and raises up.
The LORD sends poverty and wealth;
    he humbles and he exalts.
He raises the poor from the dust
    and lifts the needy from the ash heap;
he seats them with princes
    and has them inherit a throne of honor.

EPHESIANS 1:11

In him we were also chosen, having been predestined according to the plan of him who works out everything in conformity with the purpose of his will.

When have you questioned God's purposes in your life? Talk with Him about it, asking Him to help you trust that He is accomplishing His will in the world.

JANUARY 23

God's Irresistible Will

PSALM 115:2–3

> Why do the nations say,
>   "Where is their God?"
> Our God is in heaven;
>   he does whatever pleases him.

JOB 9:12, 14

> If he snatches away, who can stop him?
>   Who can say to him, "What are you doing?" . . .
> How then can I dispute with him?
>   How can I find words to argue with him?

ROMANS 9:19–21

One of you will say to me: "Then why does God still blame us? For who is able to resist his will?" But who are you, a human being, to talk back to God? "Shall what is formed say to the one who formed it, 'Why did you make me like this?'" Does not the potter have the right to make out of the same lump of clay some pottery for special purposes and some for common use?

Lord, nothing can stop you from doing what you want to do.
Thank you that even when I don't understand what you're doing,
I can know that you are acting in perfect wisdom.

God's Will on Earth

PSALM 2:1–4

Why do the nations conspire
    and the peoples plot in vain?
The kings of the earth rise up
    and the rulers band together
    against the Lord and against his anointed, saying,
"Let us break their chains
    and throw off their shackles."
The One enthroned in heaven laughs;
    the Lord scoffs at them.

DANIEL 4:35

All the peoples of the earth
    are regarded as nothing.
He does as he pleases
    with the powers of heaven
    and the peoples of the earth.
No one can hold back his hand
    or say to him: "What have you done?"

MATTHEW 6:9–10

This, then, is how you should pray:

"Our Father in heaven,
hallowed be your name,
your kingdom come,
your will be done,
    on earth as it is in heaven."

No matter who or what opposes God, He is bringing His kingdom on earth as it is in heaven.

God's Will through His Servants

PSALM 103:20–22

Praise the LORD, you his angels,
    you mighty ones who do his bidding,
    who obey his word.
Praise the LORD, all his heavenly hosts,
    you his servants who do his will.
Praise the LORD, all his works
    everywhere in his dominion.

ISAIAH 44:24, 28

I am the LORD,
    the Maker of all things,
    who stretches out the heavens,
    who spreads out the earth by myself, . . .
who says of Cyrus, "He is my shepherd
    and will accomplish all that I please;
he will say of Jerusalem, 'Let it be rebuilt,'
    and of the temple, 'Let its foundations be laid.'"

EPHESIANS 5:15–18, 20

Be very careful, then, how you live—not as unwise but as wise, making the most of every opportunity, because the days are evil. Therefore do not be foolish, but understand what the Lord's will is. Do not get drunk on wine, which leads to debauchery. Instead, be filled with the Spirit, . . . always giving thanks to God the Father for everything, in the name of our Lord Jesus Christ.

When have you seen God's will accomplished through another person, maybe even someone who wasn't seeking to do God's will? Give praise to God that He is able to orchestrate all things.

God's Will against Sin

PSALM 107:33–36

He turned rivers into a desert,
    flowing springs into thirsty ground,
and fruitful land into a salt waste,
    because of the wickedness of those who lived there.
He turned the desert into pools of water
    and the parched ground into flowing springs;
there he brought the hungry to live,
    and they founded a city where they could settle.

LAMENTATIONS 3:37–39

Who can speak and have it happen
    if the Lord has not decreed it?
Is it not from the mouth of the Most High
    that both calamities and good things come?
Why should the living complain
    when punished for their sins?

1 PETER 2:15–16

For it is God's will that by doing good you should silence the ignorant talk of foolish people. Live as free people, but do not use your freedom as a cover-up for evil; live as God's slaves.

Lord, I know there is sin in my life that conflicts with your good and perfect will. Please share your wisdom with me and teach me your ways.

God's Will and Human Will

PSALM 33:10–11

> The Lord foils the plans of the nations;
>> he thwarts the purposes of the peoples.
> But the plans of the Lord stand firm forever,
>> the purposes of his heart through all generations.

PROVERBS 21:1–2

> In the Lord's hand the king's heart is a stream of water
>> that he channels toward all who please him.
> A person may think their own ways are right,
>> but the Lord weighs the heart.

LUKE 22:39–42

Jesus went out as usual to the Mount of Olives, and his disciples followed him. On reaching the place, he said to them, "Pray that you will not fall into temptation." He withdrew about a stone's throw beyond them, knelt down and prayed, "Father, if you are willing, take this cup from me; yet not my will, but yours be done."

~~

The will of God will be done. He invites you to submit your will to His and join Him in His wise purposes.

God's Will over Everything

PSALM 24:1–2

The earth is the LORD's, and everything in it,
    the world, and all who live in it;
for he founded it on the seas
    and established it on the waters.

JOB 34:13–15

Who appointed him over the earth?
    Who put him in charge of the whole world?
If it were his intention
    and he withdrew his spirit and breath,
all humanity would perish together
    and mankind would return to the dust.

REVELATION 4:11

You are worthy, our Lord and God,
    to receive glory and honor and power,
for you created all things,
    and by your will they were created
    and have their being.

~~~~~~

Does an area of your life feel beyond God's control? Take a deep breath and remember that God created everything and is in charge of everything.

God's All-Seeing Wisdom

PSALM 94:7–9

They say, "The LORD does not see;
>   the God of Jacob takes no notice."

Take notice, you senseless ones among the people;
>   you fools, when will you become wise?
Does he who fashioned the ear not hear?
>   Does he who formed the eye not see?

ISAIAH 29:15

Woe to those who go to great depths
>   to hide their plans from the LORD,
who do their work in darkness and think,
>   "Who sees us? Who will know?"

1 JOHN 3:20–22

If our hearts condemn us, we know that God is greater than our hearts, and he knows everything. Dear friends, if our hearts do not condemn us, we have confidence before God and receive from him anything we ask, because we keep his commands and do what pleases him.

Lord, you created sight and hearing, minds and hearts. Thank you for knowing and seeing me completely.

God's World-Encompassing Wisdom

PSALM 46:7–9

> The Lord Almighty is with us;
>> the God of Jacob is our fortress.
>
> Come and see what the Lord has done,
>> the desolations he has brought on the earth.
> He makes wars cease
>> to the ends of the earth.
> He breaks the bow and shatters the spear;
>> he burns the shields with fire.

JOB 28:23–24

> God understands the way to [wisdom]
>> and he alone knows where it dwells,
> for he views the ends of the earth
>> and sees everything under the heavens.

EPHESIANS 1:8–10

With all wisdom and understanding, he made known to us the mystery of his will according to his good pleasure, which he purposed in Christ, to be put into effect when the times reach their fulfillment—to bring unity to all things in heaven and on earth under Christ.

~~~

There is no thing, place, or person in the universe that God doesn't know entirely.

God's Wisdom in All Things

PSALM 104:2–4

The LORD wraps himself in light as with a garment;
    he stretches out the heavens like a tent
    and lays the beams of his upper chambers on their waters.
He makes the clouds his chariot
    and rides on the wings of the wind.
He makes winds his messengers,
    flames of fire his servants.

PROVERBS 3:19–20

By wisdom the LORD laid the earth's foundations,
    by understanding he set the heavens in place;
by his knowledge the watery depths were divided,
    and the clouds let drop the dew.

EPHESIANS 4:4–6

There is one body and one Spirit, just as you were called to one hope when you were called; one Lord, one faith, one baptism; one God and Father of all, who is over all and through all and in all.

Today, where do you see God's wisdom woven into the very fabric of His creation? Thank Him for His wisdom that holds all things in existence.

Holy

Holy, holy, holy! Lord God Almighty!

Early in the morning our song shall rise to thee.

Holy, holy, holy, merciful and mighty!

God in three persons, blessed Trinity!

Holy, holy, holy! All the saints adore thee,
casting down their golden crowns around
    the glassy sea;
cherubim and seraphim falling down before thee,
which wert and art and evermore shalt be.

Holy, holy, holy! Though the darkness hide thee,
though the eye of sinful man thy glory may not see,
only thou art holy; there is none beside thee,
perfect in pow'r, in love, and purity.

Holy, holy, holy! Lord God Almighty!
All thy works shall praise thy name in earth
    and sky and sea.
Holy, holy, holy, merciful and mighty!
God in three persons, blessed Trinity!

Reginald Heber, 1826

The Holy God Enthroned

PSALM 22:3–5

Yet you are enthroned as the Holy One;
   you are the one Israel praises.
In you our ancestors put their trust;
   they trusted and you delivered them.
To you they cried out and were saved;
   in you they trusted and were not put to shame.

ISAIAH 6:1–3

I saw the Lord, high and exalted, seated on a throne; and the train of his robe filled the temple. Above him were seraphim, each with six wings: With two wings they covered their faces, with two they covered their feet, and with two they were flying. And they were calling to one another:

"Holy, holy, holy is the LORD Almighty;
   the whole earth is full of his glory."

REVELATION 4:6, 8

In the center, around the throne, were four living creatures, and they were covered with eyes, in front and in back. . . . Day and night they never stop saying:

"'Holy, holy, holy
is the Lord God Almighty,'
who was, and is, and is to come."

~~~

Lord, you alone are completely holy, pure, separate, and other. It only makes sense for all creation to fall before your throne and worship.

God's Matchless Holiness

PSALM 77:13–15

Your ways, God, are holy.
What god is as great as our God?
You are the God who performs miracles;
you display your power among the peoples.
With your mighty arm you redeemed your people,
the descendants of Jacob and Joseph.

ISAIAH 40:25–26

"To whom will you compare me?
Or who is my equal?" says the Holy One.
Lift up your eyes and look to the heavens:
Who created all these?
He who brings out the starry host one by one
and calls forth each of them by name.

HEBREWS 7:26–28

Such a high priest truly meets our need—one who is holy, blameless, pure, set apart from sinners, exalted above the heavens. Unlike the other high priests, he does not need to offer sacrifices day after day, first for his own sins, and then for the sins of the people. He sacrificed for their sins once for all when he offered himself. For the law appoints as high priests men in all their weakness; but the oath, which came after the law, appointed the Son, who has been made perfect forever.

In His perfection, miraculous power, and sovereignty over creation, God is unmatched by any other being.

Set Apart for God's Holiness

PSALM 106:47

Save us, LORD our God,
　　and gather us from the nations,
that we may give thanks to your holy name
　　and glory in your praise.

LEVITICUS 11:44–45

I am the LORD your God; consecrate yourselves and be holy, because
I am holy. Do not make yourselves unclean by any creature that moves
along the ground. I am the LORD, who brought you up out of Egypt to
be your God; therefore be holy, because I am holy.

2 CORINTHIANS 6:17–7:1

Therefore,

"Come out from them and be separate, says the Lord.
Touch no unclean thing, and I will receive you."

And,

"I will be a Father to you,
　　and you will be my sons and daughters. . . ."

Therefore, since we have these promises, dear friends, let us purify
ourselves from everything that contaminates body and spirit, perfecting
holiness out of reverence for God.

*Where in your relationships can you practice setting yourself apart for
God? Ask your Holy Father, who gathers you to himself to purify you.*

God's Holy Dwelling

PSALM 5:4–5, 7

> For you are not a God who is pleased with wickedness;
>> with you, evil people are not welcome.
> The arrogant cannot stand
>> in your presence. . . .
> But I, by your great love,
>> can come into your house;
> in reverence I bow down
>> toward your holy temple.

OBADIAH 17–18

> But on Mount Zion will be deliverance;
>> it will be holy,
>> and Jacob will possess his inheritance.
> Jacob will be a fire
>> and Joseph a flame.

1 CORINTHIANS 3:16–17

Don't you know that you yourselves are God's temple and that God's Spirit dwells in your midst? . . . For God's temple is sacred, and you together are that temple.

~~~~

Lord, being your temple—a part of the body of Christ—is a humbling privilege. Thank you for working among your people to make our hearts and bodies a holy dwelling for your Spirit.

Priests for God's Holiness

PSALM 96:9–10

Worship the LORD in the splendor of his holiness;
    tremble before him, all the earth.
Say among the nations, "The LORD reigns."
    The world is firmly established, it cannot be moved;
    he will judge the peoples with equity.

DEUTERONOMY 7:5–6

This is what you are to do to them: Break down their altars, smash their sacred stones, cut down their Asherah poles and burn their idols in the fire. For you are a people holy to the LORD your God. The LORD your God has chosen you out of all the peoples on the face of the earth to be his people, his treasured possession.

1 PETER 2:9–10

But you are a chosen people, a royal priesthood, a holy nation, God's special possession, that you may declare the praises of him who called you out of darkness into his wonderful light. Once you were not a people, but now you are the people of God; once you had not received mercy, but now you have received mercy.

Being God's holy people means testifying to His redemption power and showing others what it looks like to live in right relationship with Him and with others.

God's Holy Grace

PSALM 103:1–4

> Praise the LORD, my soul;
>> all my inmost being, praise his holy name.
> Praise the LORD, my soul,
>> and forget not all his benefits—
> who forgives all your sins
>> and heals all your diseases,
> who redeems your life from the pit
>> and crowns you with love and compassion.

HOSEA 11:9–10

> I will not carry out my fierce anger,
>> nor will I devastate Ephraim again.
> For I am God, and not a man—
>> the Holy One among you.
>> I will not come against their cities.
> They will follow the LORD;
>> he will roar like a lion.
> When he roars,
>> his children will come trembling from the west.

COLOSSIANS 1:21–23

Once you were alienated from God and were enemies in your minds because of your evil behavior. But now he has reconciled you by Christ's physical body through death to present you holy in his sight, without blemish and free from accusation—if you continue in your faith, established and firm, and do not move from the hope held out in the gospel.

When was a time that you have experienced God's forgiveness and unique grace? Thank God that He isn't like us.

God's Holy Relationships

PSALM 99:9

> Exalt the LORD our God
>> and worship at his holy mountain,
>> for the LORD our God is holy.

LEVITICUS 20:23, 26

You must not live according to the customs of the nations I am going to drive out before you. . . .

You are to be holy to me because I, the LORD, am holy, and I have set you apart from the nations to be my own.

HEBREWS 12:14–16

Make every effort to live in peace with everyone and to be holy; without holiness no one will see the Lord. See to it that no one falls short of the grace of God and that no bitter root grows up to cause trouble and defile many. See that no one is sexually immoral, or is godless like Esau, who for a single meal sold his inheritance rights as the oldest son.

~~~~~

Lord, it's humbling that you want me to be holy like you. Please teach me your peace and grace. Lead me away from bitterness, misusing my body, and living like you don't exist.

I Am Who I Am

PSALM 81:8–10

Hear me, my people, and I will warn you—
>if you would only listen to me, Israel!

You shall have no foreign god among you;
>you shall not worship any god other than me.

I am the LORD your God,
>who brought you up out of Egypt.

Open wide your mouth and I will fill it.

EXODUS 3:14–15

God said to Moses, "I AM WHO I AM. This is what you are to say to the Israelites: 'I AM has sent me to you.'"

God also said to Moses, "Say to the Israelites, 'The LORD, the God of your fathers—the God of Abraham, the God of Isaac and the God of Jacob—has sent me to you.'

"This is my name forever,
>the name you shall call me
>from generation to generation."

JOHN 8:56–58

"Your father Abraham rejoiced at the thought of seeing my day; he saw it and was glad."

"You are not yet fifty years old," they said to him, "and you have seen Abraham!"

"Very truly I tell you," Jesus answered, "before Abraham was born, I am!"

~~~~~

God was and is and always will be. He is uncreated, eternal, and self-defining.

I Am He

PSALM 46:10

> He says, "Be still, and know that I am God;
>> I will be exalted among the nations,
>> I will be exalted in the earth."

ISAIAH 43:11–12

> "I, even I, am the LORD,
>> and apart from me there is no savior.
> I have revealed and saved and proclaimed—
>> I, and not some foreign god among you.
> You are my witnesses," declares the LORD, "that I am God."

JOHN 4:13–14, 25–26

Jesus answered, "Everyone who drinks this water will be thirsty again, but whoever drinks the water I give them will never thirst. Indeed, the water I give them will become in them a spring of water welling up to eternal life." . . .

The woman said, "I know that Messiah" (called Christ) "is coming. When he comes, he will explain everything to us."

Then Jesus declared, "I, the one speaking to you—I am he."

What feels loud, overwhelming, or out of control today? Pause to be still before God, remembering that He is God and you are not.

I Am and Was and Am to Come

PSALM 83:18

> Let them know that you, whose name is the LORD—
> that you alone are the Most High over all the earth.

ISAIAH 44:6–7

> This is what the LORD says—
> Israel's King and Redeemer, the LORD Almighty:
> I am the first and I am the last;
> apart from me there is no God.
> Who then is like me? Let him proclaim it.
> Let him declare and lay out before me.

REVELATION 1:7–8

> "Look, he is coming with the clouds,"
> and "every eye will see him,
> even those who pierced him";
> and all peoples on earth "will mourn because of him."
> So shall it be! Amen.

"I am the Alpha and the Omega," says the Lord God, "who is, and who was, and who is to come, the Almighty."

~~~~

Lord, you were God before anything else existed, and you will be God for all eternity. Thank you for being God over my past, present, and future.

I Am the Light of the World

PSALM 118:26–27

Blessed is he who comes in the name of the LORD.
From the house of the LORD we bless you.
The LORD is God,
and he has made his light shine on us.
With boughs in hand, join in the festal procession
up to the horns of the altar.

ISAIAH 45:5–7

I am the LORD, and there is no other;
apart from me there is no God.
I will strengthen you,
though you have not acknowledged me,
so that from the rising of the sun
to the place of its setting
people may know there is none besides me.
I am the LORD, and there is no other.
I form the light and create darkness,
I bring prosperity and create disaster;
I, the LORD, do all these things.

JOHN 8:12

When Jesus spoke again to the people, he said, "I am the light of
the world. Whoever follows me will never walk in darkness, but will
have the light of life."

~~~

*God is light. He alone brings life and meaning, and in Him we see
all things as they truly are.*

I Am the Good Shepherd

PSALM 100:1–3

Shout for joy to the LORD, all the earth.
>Worship the LORD with gladness;
>come before him with joyful songs.
Know that the LORD is God.
>It is he who made us, and we are his;
>we are his people, the sheep of his pasture.

ISAIAH 40:10–11

See, the Sovereign LORD comes with power,
>and he rules with a mighty arm.
See, his reward is with him,
>and his recompense accompanies him.
He tends his flock like a shepherd:
>He gathers the lambs in his arms
and carries them close to his heart;
>he gently leads those that have young.

JOHN 10:14–15

I am the good shepherd; I know my sheep and my sheep know me—just as the Father knows me and I know the Father—and I lay down my life for the sheep.

~~~~~

What word or phrase from the passages above stood out to you? Pause to talk with God about it.

I Am the Bread of Life

PSALM 78:18–20

They willfully put God to the test
     by demanding the food they craved.
They spoke against God;
     they said, "Can God really
     spread a table in the wilderness?
True, he struck the rock,
     and water gushed out,
     streams flowed abundantly,
but can he also give us bread?
     Can he supply meat for his people?"

EXODUS 16:14–16

When the dew was gone, thin flakes like frost on the ground appeared on the desert floor. When the Israelites saw it, they said to each other, "What is it?" . . .

Moses said to them, "It is the bread the LORD has given you to eat. This is what the LORD has commanded: 'Everyone is to gather as much as they need.'"

JOHN 6:32–35

Jesus said to them, "Very truly I tell you, it is not Moses who has given you the bread from heaven, but it is my Father who gives you the true bread from heaven. For the bread of God is the bread that comes down from heaven and gives life to the world."

"Sir," they said, "always give us this bread."

Then Jesus declared, "I am the bread of life. Whoever comes to me will never go hungry."

〜〜〜

Lord, I can't live without you. Give me what I need for today. Help my unbelief when I feel like you can't satisfy me. You alone sustain all things.

I Am Salvation

PSALM 35:2–3

Take up shield and armor;
  arise and come to my aid.
Brandish spear and javelin
  against those who pursue me.
Say to me,
  "I am your salvation."

EXODUS 15:2–3

The LORD is my strength and my defense;
  he has become my salvation.
He is my God, and I will praise him,
  my father's God, and I will exalt him.
The LORD is a warrior;
  the LORD is his name.

JOHN 11:25–27

Jesus said to her, "I am the resurrection and the life. The one who believes in me will live, even though they die; and whoever lives by believing in me will never die. Do you believe this?"

"Yes, Lord," she replied, "I believe that you are the Messiah, the Son of God, who is to come into the world."

～～～

God is the only one who can rescue you from the sin, separation, sickness, and death we all experience in this life.

The Only Self-Existent One

PSALM 90:1–2

Lord, you have been our dwelling place
    throughout all generations.
Before the mountains were born
    or you brought forth the whole world,
    from everlasting to everlasting you are God.

NEHEMIAH 9:5–6

Blessed be your glorious name, and may it be exalted above all blessing and praise. You alone are the LORD. You made the heavens, even the highest heavens, and all their starry host, the earth and all that is on it, the seas and all that is in them. You give life to everything, and the multitudes of heaven worship you.

ACTS 17:25

He is not served by human hands, as if he needed anything. Rather, he himself gives everyone life and breath and everything else.

What is one thing you rely on that you're grateful God has given to you? Thank Him that He provides for you out of His own boundless existence.

The Only Uncreated God

PSALM 102:25–26

> In the beginning you laid the foundations of the earth,
>> and the heavens are the work of your hands.
> They will perish, but you remain;
>> they will all wear out like a garment.
> Like clothing you will change them
>> and they will be discarded.

ISAIAH 45:20–21

> Ignorant are those who carry about idols of wood,
>> who pray to gods that cannot save.
> Declare what is to be, present it—
>> let them take counsel together.
> Who foretold this long ago,
>> who declared it from the distant past?
> Was it not I, the LORD?
>> And there is no God apart from me,
> a righteous God and a Savior;
>> there is none but me.

JOHN 17:4–5

I have brought you glory on earth by finishing the work you gave me to do. And now, Father, glorify me in your presence with the glory I had with you before the world began.

〜〜〜

Lord, I can't fully comprehend you. You are uncreated, limitless, without age or deterioration. Teach me to always keep in mind your glory.

The Only Fountain of Life

PSALM 36:7–9

How priceless is your unfailing love, O God!
     People take refuge in the shadow of your wings.
They feast on the abundance of your house;
     you give them drink from your river of delights.
For with you is the fountain of life;
     in your light we see light.

ISAIAH 48:12–13

Listen to me, Jacob,
     Israel, whom I have called:
I am he;
     I am the first and I am the last.
My own hand laid the foundations of the earth,
     and my right hand spread out the heavens;
when I summon them,
     they all stand up together.

JOHN 5:25–26

Very truly I tell you, a time is coming and has now come when the
dead will hear the voice of the Son of God and those who hear will live.
For as the Father has life in himself, so he has granted the Son also to
have life in himself.

~~~

*All life springs from the life that God—Father, Son, and Holy Spirit
in eternal community—has always had within himself.*

The Only Source of Being

PSALM 90:3, 5–6

> You turn people back to dust,
>> saying, "Return to dust, you mortals."...
>
> Yet you sweep people away in the sleep of death—
>> they are like the new grass of the morning:
> In the morning it springs up new,
>> but by evening it is dry and withered.

HABAKKUK 1:12

> LORD, are you not from everlasting?
>> My God, my Holy One, you will never die.

HEBREWS 2:10

> In bringing many sons and daughters to glory, it was fitting that God, for whom and through whom everything exists, should make the pioneer of their salvation perfect through what he suffered.

~~~~~~

When was a time that you clearly saw God's power over life and death? Thank God that all things exist for Him and through Him.

The Only Sustainer of Creation

PSALM 93:1–2

> The Lord reigns, he is robed in majesty;
> > the Lord is robed in majesty and armed with strength;
> > indeed, the world is established, firm and secure.
> Your throne was established long ago;
> > you are from all eternity.

JOB 38:4–7

> Where were you when I laid the earth's foundation?
> > Tell me, if you understand.
> Who marked off its dimensions? Surely you know!
> > Who stretched a measuring line across it?
> On what were its footings set,
> > or who laid its cornerstone—
> while the morning stars sang together
> > and all the angels shouted for joy?

1 CORINTHIANS 8:6

> Yet for us there is but one God, the Father, from whom all things came and for whom we live; and there is but one Lord, Jesus Christ, through whom all things came and through whom we live.

~~~~

Lord, your ability to create and sustain all things is too marvelous for me. All creation is from you and through you. Thank you for blessing me with people, places, and things that you love too.

The Only King of All

PSALM 102:27–28

But you remain the same,
and your years will never end.
The children of your servants will live in your presence;
their descendants will be established before you.

DANIEL 4:34

Then I praised the Most High; I honored and glorified him who
lives forever.

His dominion is an eternal dominion;
his kingdom endures from generation to generation.

1 TIMOTHY 6:13–16

I charge you to keep this command without spot or blame until the
appearing of our Lord Jesus Christ, which God will bring about in his
own time—God, the blessed and only Ruler, the King of kings and Lord
of lords, who alone is immortal and who lives in unapproachable light,
whom no one has seen or can see. To him be honor and might forever.
Amen.

~~~~~~

*God is the true King over all people. His reign of holiness and love will
be for ever and ever.*

The Only God for All Time

PSALM 146:3–6

> Do not put your trust in princes,
>   in human beings, who cannot save.
> When their spirit departs, they return to the ground;
>   on that very day their plans come to nothing.
> Blessed are those whose help is the God of Jacob,
>   whose hope is in the LORD their God.
>
> He is the Maker of heaven and earth,
>   the sea, and everything in them.

ISAIAH 41:4

> Who has done this and carried it through,
>   calling forth the generations from the beginning?
> I, the LORD—with the first of them
>   and with the last—I am he.

REVELATION 1:17–18

> When I saw him, I fell at his feet as though dead. Then he placed his right hand on me and said: "Do not be afraid. I am the First and the Last. I am the Living One; I was dead, and now look, I am alive for ever and ever! And I hold the keys of death and Hades."

———

What is something in your future that worries you? Ask God to remind you that as He has sustained all things in the past, so He will in the future.

God's Complete Self-Sufficiency

PSALM 50:9–11

I have no need of a bull from your stall
    or of goats from your pens,
for every animal of the forest is mine,
    and the cattle on a thousand hills.
I know every bird in the mountains,
    and the insects in the fields are mine.

JOB 12:7–10

But ask the animals, and they will teach you,
    or the birds in the sky, and they will tell you;
or speak to the earth, and it will teach you,
    or let the fish in the sea inform you.
Which of all these does not know
    that the hand of the LORD has done this?
In his hand is the life of every creature
    and the breath of all mankind.

2 TIMOTHY 1:9–10

He has saved us and called us to a holy life—not because of anything we have done but because of his own purpose and grace. This grace was given us in Christ Jesus before the beginning of time, but it has now been revealed through the appearing of our Savior, Christ Jesus.

～～

Lord, you don't need anything from me; everything already belongs to you. Thank you for calling me into holy relationship with you because of your own purpose and grace.

God's Eternal Sufficiency
within the Trinity

PSALM 95:3–5

> For the LORD is the great God,
>> the great King above all gods.
> In his hand are the depths of the earth,
>> and the mountain peaks belong to him.
> The sea is his, for he made it,
>> and his hands formed the dry land.

PROVERBS 30:1–4

> I am weary, God,
>> but I can prevail.
> Surely I am only a brute, not a man;
>> I do not have human understanding.
> I have not learned wisdom,
>> nor have I attained to the knowledge of the Holy One.
> Who has gone up to heaven and come down?
>> Whose hands have gathered up the wind?
> Who has wrapped up the waters in a cloak?
>> Who has established all the ends of the earth?
> What is his name, and what is the name of his son?
>> Surely you know!

JOHN 1:1–2

In the beginning was the Word, and the Word was with God, and the Word was God. He was with God in the beginning.

～～～

God does not need creation. He has always had everything He needs within the eternal relationship of Father, Son, and Holy Spirit.

God's Provision from His Sufficiency

PSALM 65:9–11

> You care for the land and water it;
>> you enrich it abundantly.
> The streams of God are filled with water
>> to provide the people with grain,
>> for so you have ordained it.
> You drench its furrows and level its ridges;
>> you soften it with showers and bless its crops.
> You crown the year with your bounty,
>> and your carts overflow with abundance.

EXODUS 16:11–12

The LORD said to Moses, "I have heard the grumbling of the Israelites. Tell them, 'At twilight you will eat meat, and in the morning you will be filled with bread. Then you will know that I am the LORD your God.'"

PHILIPPIANS 4:19–20

And my God will meet all your needs according to the riches of his glory in Christ Jesus. To our God and Father be glory for ever and ever. Amen.

Where do you see God's everyday provision in your life? Thank Him for meeting your needs out of the richness of himself.

The Sufficiency of God's Rule

PSALM 93:3–5

> The seas have lifted up, LORD,
>> the seas have lifted up their voice;
>> the seas have lifted up their pounding waves.
> Mightier than the thunder of the great waters,
>> mightier than the breakers of the sea—
>> the Lord on high is mighty.
>
> Your statutes, LORD, stand firm;
>> holiness adorns your house
>> for endless days.

DANIEL 6:26–27

> For he is the living God
>> and he endures forever;
> his kingdom will not be destroyed,
>> his dominion will never end.
> He rescues and he saves;
>> he performs signs and wonders
>> in the heavens and on the earth.

MATTHEW 6:31–34

So do not worry, saying, "What shall we eat?" or "What shall we drink?" or "What shall we wear?" For the pagans run after all these things, and your heavenly Father knows that you need them. But seek first his kingdom and his righteousness, and all these things will be given to you as well. Therefore do not worry about tomorrow, for tomorrow will worry about itself.

Lord, I often think that I know best how things should be run. Please teach me to trust that you alone know how best to rule all things.

The Sufficiency of God's Rescue

PSALM 40:16–17

But may all who seek you
rejoice and be glad in you;
may those who long for your saving help always say,
"The LORD is great!"

But as for me, I am poor and needy;
may the Lord think of me.
You are my help and my deliverer;
you are my God, do not delay.

DEUTERONOMY 32:39

See now that I myself am he!
There is no god besides me.
I put to death and I bring to life,
I have wounded and I will heal,
and no one can deliver out of my hand.

ACTS 4:11–12

Jesus is

"the stone you builders rejected,
which has become the cornerstone."

Salvation is found in no one else, for there is no other name under
heaven given to mankind by which we must be saved.

~~~~~~

*God saves His people in His time and in His way. His salvation is
enough for you.*

Creation out of God's Self-Sufficiency

PSALM 139:13–15

> For you created my inmost being;
>> you knit me together in my mother's womb.
> I praise you because I am fearfully and wonderfully made;
>> your works are wonderful,
>> I know that full well.
> My frame was not hidden from you
>> when I was made in the secret place,
>> when I was woven together in the depths of the earth.

GENESIS 2:7

Then the LORD God formed a man from the dust of the ground and breathed into his nostrils the breath of life, and the man became a living being.

ACTS 17:28

"For in him we live and move and have our being." As some of your own poets have said, "We are his offspring."

~~~

Is there an aspect of yourself or your body that sometimes feels like a mistake? Talk with God about it, asking Him to remind you that He creates and sustains life from His own boundless life.

All-Sufficient without Our Sacrifices

PSALM 51:15–16

> Open my lips, Lord,
>> and my mouth will declare your praise.
> You do not delight in sacrifice, or I would bring it;
>> you do not take pleasure in burnt offerings.

ISAIAH 1:11–13

> "The multitude of your sacrifices—
>> what are they to me?" says the LORD. . . .
> "I have no pleasure
>> in the blood of bulls and lambs and goats.
> When you come to appear before me,
>> who has asked this of you,
>> this trampling of my courts?
> Stop bringing meaningless offerings!"

HEBREWS 10:5–7

Therefore, when Christ came into the world, he said:

> "Sacrifice and offering you did not desire,
>> but a body you prepared for me;
> with burnt offerings and sin offerings
>> you were not pleased.
> Then I said, 'Here I am—it is written about me in the scroll—
>> I have come to do your will, my God.'"

Lord, you don't need any of my attempts to appease you or impress you. Please teach me that you are already complete without anything I do for you.

God Is Holy

PSALM 29:2–4

Worship the LORD in the splendor of his holiness.

The voice of the LORD is over the waters;
    the God of glory thunders,
    the LORD thunders over the mighty waters.
The voice of the LORD is powerful;
    the voice of the LORD is majestic.

EXODUS 15:11

Who among the gods
    is like you, LORD?
Who is like you—
    majestic in holiness,
awesome in glory,
    working wonders?

REVELATION 15:3–4

Great and marvelous are your deeds,
    Lord God Almighty.
Just and true are your ways,
    King of the nations.
Who will not fear you, Lord,
    and bring glory to your name?
For you alone are holy.
All nations will come
    and worship before you.

~~~~~

God is the one and only God. His power, glory, and majesty are unique and without rival.

Merciful

Amazing grace, how sweet the sound

that saved a wretch like me!

I once was lost, but now am found,

was blind, but now I see.

'Twas grace that taught my heart to fear,
and grace my fears relieved;
how precious did that grace appear
the hour I first believed!

Through many dangers, toils, and snares
I have already come:
'tis grace has brought me safe thus far,
and grace will lead me home.

The Lord has promised good to me,
His word my hope secures;
He will my shield and portion be
as long as life endures.

John Newton, 1789

God's Eternal Mercy

PSALM 25:6–7

> Remember, Lord, your great mercy and love,
>   for they are from of old.
> Do not remember the sins of my youth
>   and my rebellious ways;
> according to your love remember me,
>   for you, Lord, are good.

ISAIAH 63:8–9

> He said, "Surely they are my people,
>   children who will be true to me";
>   and so he became their Savior.
> In all their distress he too was distressed,
>   and the angel of his presence saved them.
> In his love and mercy he redeemed them;
>   he lifted them up and carried them
>   all the days of old.

LUKE 1:50, 54–55

> His mercy extends to those who fear him,
>   from generation to generation. . . .
> He has helped his servant Israel,
>   remembering to be merciful
> to Abraham and his descendants forever,
>   just as he promised our ancestors.

What reminds you of God's mercies in your life? How have you seen His mercy to others around you or in your community of believers?

The God Who Reveals His Mercy

PSALM 27:7–9

Hear my voice when I call, Lord;
    be merciful to me and answer me.
My heart says of you, "Seek his face!"
    Your face, Lord, I will seek.
Do not hide your face from me,
    do not turn your servant away in anger;
    you have been my helper.
Do not reject me or forsake me,
    God my Savior.

EXODUS 33:18–19

Then Moses said, "Now show me your glory."

And the Lord said, "I will cause all my goodness to pass in front of you, and I will proclaim my name, the Lord, in your presence. I will have mercy on whom I will have mercy, and I will have compassion on whom I will have compassion."

ROMANS 9:14–16

What then shall we say? Is God unjust? Not at all! For he says to Moses,

"I will have mercy on whom I have mercy,
    and I will have compassion on whom I have compassion."

It does not, therefore, depend on human desire or effort, but on God's mercy.

Lord, sometimes I forget your mercy and think my pain means that you're against me. Show yourself to me; I want to see who you are.

God's Mercy with Our Sin

PSALM 51:1–2

Have mercy on me, O God,
　　according to your unfailing love;
according to your great compassion
　　blot out my transgressions.
Wash away all my iniquity
　　and cleanse me from my sin.

MICAH 7:18–20

Who is a God like you,
　　who pardons sin and forgives the transgression
　　of the remnant of his inheritance?
You do not stay angry forever
　　but delight to show mercy.
You will again have compassion on us;
　　you will tread our sins underfoot
　　and hurl all our iniquities into the depths of the sea.
You will be faithful to Jacob,
　　and show love to Abraham,
as you pledged on oath to our ancestors
　　in days long ago.

TITUS 3:3–5

At one time we too were foolish, disobedient, deceived and enslaved by all kinds of passions and pleasures. We lived in malice and envy, being hated and hating one another. But when the kindness and love of God our Savior appeared, he saved us, not because of righteous things we had done, but because of his mercy.

~~~~~

God saves us out of His mercy because He is kind, compassionate, and loving.

God's Mercy to His Chosen People

PSALM 135:13–14

Your name, LORD, endures forever,
    your renown, LORD, through all generations.
For the LORD will vindicate his people
    and have compassion on his servants.

DEUTERONOMY 4:30–31

When you are in distress and all these things have happened to you, then in later days you will return to the LORD your God and obey him. For the LORD your God is a merciful God; he will not abandon or destroy you or forget the covenant with your ancestors, which he confirmed to them by oath.

1 PETER 1:3–5

Praise be to the God and Father of our Lord Jesus Christ! In his great mercy he has given us new birth into a living hope through the resurrection of Jesus Christ from the dead, and into an inheritance that can never perish, spoil or fade. This inheritance is kept in heaven for you, who through faith are shielded by God's power until the coming of the salvation that is ready to be revealed in the last time.

In what area of your life do you need to return to God? Talk with Him about it, asking Him to show you the depths of His mercy and your living hope in Jesus Christ.

God's Mercy through His Chosen People

PSALM 30:8–9

To you, Lord, I called;
>to the Lord I cried for mercy:
"What is gained if I am silenced,
>if I go down to the pit?
Will the dust praise you?
>Will it proclaim your faithfulness?"

MICAH 6:7–8

Will the Lord be pleased with thousands of rams,
>with ten thousand rivers of olive oil?
Shall I offer my firstborn for my transgression,
>the fruit of my body for the sin of my soul?
He has shown you, O mortal, what is good.
>And what does the Lord require of you?
To act justly and to love mercy
>and to walk humbly with your God.

MATTHEW 9:10–13

While Jesus was having dinner at Matthew's house, many tax collectors and sinners came and ate with him and his disciples. When the Pharisees saw this, they asked his disciples, "Why does your teacher eat with tax collectors and sinners?"

On hearing this, Jesus said, "It is not the healthy who need a doctor, but the sick. But go and learn what this means: 'I desire mercy, not sacrifice.' For I have not come to call the righteous, but sinners."

Lord, you are merciful, and you want me to be merciful too. Help me to tell others of the mercy you've shown me, and to treat others with mercy, justice, and humility.

God's Mercy in Discipline

PSALM 77:7–9

> Will the Lord reject forever?
>> Will he never show his favor again?
> Has his unfailing love vanished forever?
>> Has his promise failed for all time?
> Has God forgotten to be merciful?
>> Has he in anger withheld his compassion?

HABAKKUK 3:2

> Lord, I have heard of your fame;
>> I stand in awe of your deeds, Lord.
> Repeat them in our day,
>> in our time make them known;
>> in wrath remember mercy.

JUDE 20–23

But you, dear friends, by building yourselves up in your most holy faith and praying in the Holy Spirit, keep yourselves in God's love as you wait for the mercy of our Lord Jesus Christ to bring you to eternal life.

Be merciful to those who doubt; save others by snatching them from the fire; to others show mercy, mixed with fear—hating even the clothing stained by corrupted flesh.

～～～

God's anger with sin can feel like rejection or betrayal, but in His mercy He is bringing you to eternal life, even when you can't see it.

God's Mercy amid Life's Brokenness

PSALM 57:1–3

> Have mercy on me, my God, have mercy on me,
>   for in you I take refuge.
> I will take refuge in the shadow of your wings
>   until the disaster has passed.
> I cry out to God Most High,
>   to God, who vindicates me.
> He sends from heaven and saves me,
>   rebuking those who hotly pursue me—
>   God sends forth his love and his faithfulness.

2 SAMUEL 24:14

David said to Gad, "I am in deep distress. Let us fall into the hands of the LORD, for his mercy is great; but do not let me fall into human hands."

HEBREWS 4:15–16

For we do not have a high priest who is unable to empathize with our weaknesses, but we have one who has been tempted in every way, just as we are—yet he did not sin. Let us then approach God's throne of grace with confidence, so that we may receive mercy and find grace to help us in our time of need.

~~~~~~

What word or phrase from the passages above stood out to you?
Pause to talk with God about it.

God's Never-Failing Compassion

PSALM 85:5–7

Will you be angry with us forever?
Will you prolong your anger through all generations?
Will you not revive us again,
that your people may rejoice in you?
Show us your unfailing love, Lord,
and grant us your salvation.

LAMENTATIONS 3:22–24

Because of the Lord's great love we are not consumed,
for his compassions never fail.
They are new every morning;
great is your faithfulness.
I say to myself, "The Lord is my portion;
therefore I will wait for him."

2 CORINTHIANS 1:3–5

Praise be to the God and Father of our Lord Jesus Christ, the
Father of compassion and the God of all comfort, who comforts us
in all our troubles, so that we can comfort those in any trouble with
the comfort we ourselves receive from God. For just as we share
abundantly in the sufferings of Christ, so also our comfort abounds
through Christ.

~~~~~

*Lord, every morning I can wake up confident that you have
compassion for me. Please help it sink in for me that there is nothing
more reliable than your compassion.*

God, Our Compassionate Parent

PSALM 72:3–4

May the mountains bring prosperity to the people,
     the hills the fruit of righteousness.
May he defend the afflicted among the people
     and save the children of the needy.

ISAIAH 49:15–16

Can a mother forget the baby at her breast
     and have no compassion on the child she has borne?
Though she may forget,
     I will not forget you!
See, I have engraved you on the palms of my hands;
     your walls are ever before me.

LUKE 15:20–24

But while he was still a long way off, his father saw him and was filled with compassion for him; he ran to his son, threw his arms around him and kissed him.

The son said to him, "Father, I have sinned against heaven and against you. I am no longer worthy to be called your son."

But the father said to his servants, "Quick! Bring the best robe and put it on him. Put a ring on his finger and sandals on his feet. Bring the fattened calf and kill it. Let's have a feast and celebrate. For this son of mine was dead and is alive again; he was lost and is found."

Whatever your experience with human parents, God has compassion on His children.

God's Compassion for His Covenant People

PSALM 102:13–14

You will arise and have compassion on Zion,
  for it is time to show favor to her;
  the appointed time has come.
For her stones are dear to your servants;
  her very dust moves them to pity.

ZECHARIAH 10:6

I will strengthen Judah
  and save the tribes of Joseph.
I will restore them
  because I have compassion on them.
They will be as though
  I had not rejected them,
for I am the LORD their God
  and I will answer them.

LUKE 1:76–79

And you, my child, will be called a prophet of the Most High;
  for you will go on before the Lord to prepare the way for him,
to give his people the knowledge of salvation
  through the forgiveness of their sins,
because of the tender mercy of our God,
  by which the rising sun will come to us from heaven
to shine on those living in darkness.

Where do you feel like God has rejected you or left you in the dark? Bring those feelings to God, asking Him to show you His tender compassion.

God's All-Inviting Compassion

PSALM 90:13–14

Relent, Lord! How long will it be?
    Have compassion on your servants.
Satisfy us in the morning with your unfailing love,
    that we may sing for joy and be glad all our days.

LAMENTATIONS 3:31–33

For no one is cast off
    by the Lord forever.
Though he brings grief, he will show compassion,
    so great is his unfailing love.
For he does not willingly bring affliction
    or grief to anyone.

LUKE 6:35–36

But love your enemies, do good to them, and lend to them without expecting to get anything back. Then your reward will be great, and you will be children of the Most High, because he is kind to the ungrateful and wicked. Be merciful, just as your Father is merciful.

Lord, you are so unlike me. You love your enemies and those who are ungrateful and wicked. You don't afflict anyone just because. Teach me to be merciful like you.

God's Compassion for Everyday Needs

PSALM 111:4–5

> He has caused his wonders to be remembered;
> the LORD is gracious and compassionate.
> He provides food for those who fear him;
> he remembers his covenant forever.

NEHEMIAH 9:19–21

Because of your great compassion you did not abandon them in the wilderness. By day the pillar of cloud did not fail to guide them on their path, nor the pillar of fire by night to shine on the way they were to take. You gave your good Spirit to instruct them. You did not withhold your manna from their mouths, and you gave them water for their thirst. For forty years you sustained them in the wilderness; they lacked nothing, their clothes did not wear out nor did their feet become swollen.

MARK 8:1–3

During those days another large crowd gathered. Since they had nothing to eat, Jesus called his disciples to him and said, "I have compassion for these people; they have already been with me three days and have nothing to eat. If I send them home hungry, they will collapse on the way, because some of them have come a long distance."

~~~~

God cares whether you're hungry or thirsty or have clothes to wear.
No need is too basic for His compassion.

God's Compassion for Those in Need

PSALM 116:5–6

The LORD is gracious and righteous;
    our God is full of compassion.
The LORD protects the unwary;
    when I was brought low, he saved me.

EXODUS 22:25–27

If you lend money to one of my people among you who is needy, do not treat it like a business deal; charge no interest. If you take your neighbor's cloak as a pledge, return it by sunset, because that cloak is the only covering your neighbor has. What else can they sleep in? When they cry out to me, I will hear, for I am compassionate.

MATTHEW 9:35–36

Jesus went through all the towns and villages, teaching in their synagogues, proclaiming the good news of the kingdom and healing every disease and sickness. When he saw the crowds, he had compassion on them, because they were harassed and helpless, like sheep without a shepherd.

How have you seen God's compassion for you when you've been in need? How can you show Christlike compassion to those in need around you?

The Compassion of God's Laws

PSALM 119:156–157

Your compassion, LORD, is great;
    preserve my life according to your laws.
Many are the foes who persecute me,
    but I have not turned from your statutes.

DEUTERONOMY 30:2–4

When you and your children return to the LORD your God and obey him with all your heart and with all your soul according to everything I command you today, then the LORD your God will restore your fortunes and have compassion on you and gather you again from all the nations where he scattered you. Even if you have been banished to the most distant land under the heavens, from there the LORD your God will gather you and bring you back.

MATTHEW 23:23–24

Woe to you, teachers of the law and Pharisees, you hypocrites! You give a tenth of your spices—mint, dill and cumin. But you have neglected the more important matters of the law—justice, mercy and faithfulness. You should have practiced the latter, without neglecting the former. You blind guides! You strain out a gnat but swallow a camel.

~~~~~

Lord, forgive me and show me your compassion when I've neglected your commands for right living. I want my relationships to be full of mercy and justice and faithfulness, as your relationships are.

God Is Slow to Anger

PSALM 103:7–10

> He made known his ways to Moses,
>   his deeds to the people of Israel:
> The LORD is compassionate and gracious,
>   slow to anger, abounding in love.
> He will not always accuse,
>   nor will he harbor his anger forever;
> he does not treat us as our sins deserve
>   or repay us according to our iniquities.

EXODUS 34:5–6

Then the LORD came down in the cloud and stood there with him and proclaimed his name, the LORD. And he passed in front of Moses, proclaiming, "The LORD, the LORD, the compassionate and gracious God, slow to anger, abounding in love and faithfulness, maintaining love to thousands, and forgiving wickedness, rebellion and sin. Yet he does not leave the guilty unpunished; he punishes the children and their children for the sin of the parents to the third and fourth generation."

2 PETER 3:8–9

But do not forget this one thing, dear friends: With the Lord a day is like a thousand years, and a thousand years are like a day. The Lord is not slow in keeping his promise, as some understand slowness. Instead he is patient with you, not wanting anyone to perish, but everyone to come to repentance.

Being slow to anger was one of the first, fundamental characteristics God revealed about himself when Moses asked to see God.

God's Brief Anger

PSALM 30:4–5

Sing the praises of the Lord, you his faithful people;
    praise his holy name.
For his anger lasts only a moment,
    but his favor lasts a lifetime;
weeping may stay for the night,
    but rejoicing comes in the morning.

ISAIAH 54:7–8

"For a brief moment I abandoned you,
    but with deep compassion I will bring you back.
In a surge of anger
    I hid my face from you for a moment,
but with everlasting kindness
    I will have compassion on you,"
    says the Lord your Redeemer.

1 CORINTHIANS 13:4–5

Love is patient, love is kind. . . . It is not easily angered, it keeps
no record of wrongs.

~~~~~

*Do you feel that God is angry about a sin in your life? Talk with Him
about it. Repent where you need to repent, remembering that His
kindness and compassion are forever.*

God's Confounding Slowness to Anger

PSALM 86:14–16

Arrogant foes are attacking me, O God;
    ruthless people are trying to kill me—
    they have no regard for you.
But you, Lord, are a compassionate and gracious God,
    slow to anger, abounding in love and faithfulness.
Turn to me and have mercy on me;
    show your strength in behalf of your servant.

JONAH 4:1–3

But to Jonah this seemed very wrong, and he became angry. He prayed to the LORD, "Isn't this what I said, LORD, when I was still at home? That is what I tried to forestall by fleeing to Tarshish. I knew that you are a gracious and compassionate God, slow to anger and abounding in love, a God who relents from sending calamity. Now, LORD, take away my life, for it is better for me to die than to live."

ROMANS 5:10–11

For if, while we were God's enemies, we were reconciled to him through the death of his Son, how much more, having been reconciled, shall we be saved through his life! Not only is this so, but we also boast in God through our Lord Jesus Christ, through whom we have now received reconciliation.

~~~~

Lord, I don't understand why you don't bring down your anger on the evil, injustice, and pride I see around me. Please help me to notice what you are doing by being slow to anger.

Living Out God's
Slowness of Anger

PSALM 145:6-8

They tell of the power of your awesome works—
and I will proclaim your great deeds.
They celebrate your abundant goodness
and joyfully sing of your righteousness.

The LORD is gracious and compassionate,
slow to anger and rich in love.

ECCLESIASTES 7:8-9

The end of a matter is better than its beginning,
and patience is better than pride.
Do not be quickly provoked in your spirit,
for anger resides in the lap of fools.

JAMES 1:19-21

My dear brothers and sisters, take note of this: Everyone should be
quick to listen, slow to speak and slow to become angry, because human
anger does not produce the righteousness that God desires. Therefore,
get rid of all moral filth and the evil that is so prevalent and humbly
accept the word planted in you, which can save you.

God is slow to anger. You can be slow to anger too.

God's Anger and God's Forgiveness

PSALM 78:38–39

> Yet he was merciful;
>> he forgave their iniquities
>> and did not destroy them.
> Time after time he restrained his anger
>> and did not stir up his full wrath.
> He remembered that they were but flesh,
>> a passing breeze that does not return.

NUMBERS 14:17–19

Now may the Lord's strength be displayed, just as you have declared: "The LORD is slow to anger, abounding in love and forgiving sin and rebellion. Yet he does not leave the guilty unpunished; he punishes the children for the sin of the parents to the third and fourth generation." In accordance with your great love, forgive the sin of these people, just as you have pardoned them from the time they left Egypt until now.

EPHESIANS 2:3–5

All of us also lived among them at one time, gratifying the cravings of our flesh and following its desires and thoughts. Like the rest, we were by nature deserving of wrath. But because of his great love for us, God, who is rich in mercy, made us alive with Christ even when we were dead in transgressions—it is by grace you have been saved.

~~~~~~

What do you feel when you stop to consider that God has forgiven you for sins that deserved His anger? Take time to thank Him for His rich mercy.

God's Slow but Just Anger

PSALM 7:6–8

Arise, Lord, in your anger;
    rise up against the rage of my enemies.
    Awake, my God; decree justice.
Let the assembled peoples gather around you,
    while you sit enthroned over them on high.
Let the Lord judge the peoples.

NAHUM 1:3–4

The Lord is slow to anger but great in power;
    the Lord will not leave the guilty unpunished.
His way is in the whirlwind and the storm,
    and clouds are the dust of his feet.
He rebukes the sea and dries it up;
    he makes all the rivers run dry.

ROMANS 2:2–4

Now we know that God's judgment against those who do such things is based on truth. So when you, a mere human being, pass judgment on them and yet do the same things, do you think you will escape God's judgment? Or do you show contempt for the riches of his kindness, forbearance and patience, not realizing that God's kindness is intended to lead you to repentance?

～～～

Lord, you are slow to anger, but you do punish the guilty. Teach me that I am not above your just judgment. Whether through your discipline or your patience, show me the harm of my sins.

The Slow Anger of the One True God

PSALM 69:16–18

Answer me, LORD, out of the goodness of your love;
    in your great mercy turn to me.
Do not hide your face from your servant;
    answer me quickly, for I am in trouble.
Come near and rescue me;
    deliver me because of my foes.

NEHEMIAH 9:17–18

They became stiff-necked and in their rebellion appointed a leader in order to return to their slavery. But you are a forgiving God, gracious and compassionate, slow to anger and abounding in love. Therefore you did not desert them, even when they cast for themselves an image of a calf and said, "This is your god, who brought you up out of Egypt," or when they committed awful blasphemies.

1 THESSALONIANS 1:9–10

They tell how you turned to God from idols to serve the living and true God, and to wait for his Son from heaven, whom he raised from the dead—Jesus, who rescues us from the coming wrath.

Even when you're chasing after other idols, God is patient and will not desert you.

The Generosity of God

PSALM 31:19

How abundant are the good things
    that you have stored up for those who fear you,
that you bestow in the sight of all,
    on those who take refuge in you.

JEREMIAH 31:10–12

"He who scattered Israel will gather them
    and will watch over his flock like a shepherd."
For the Lord will deliver Jacob
    and redeem them from the hand of those stronger than they.
They will come and shout for joy on the heights of Zion;
    they will rejoice in the bounty of the Lord—
the grain, the new wine and the olive oil,
    the young of the flocks and herds.
They will be like a well-watered garden,
    and they will sorrow no more.

ROMANS 8:31–32

What, then, shall we say in response to these things? If God is for us, who can be against us? He who did not spare his own Son, but gave him up for us all—how will he not also, along with him, graciously give us all things?

~~~

Is there an area of your life that feels depleted or lacking? Ask God to remind you of the generosity He has shown you, starting with the gift of His Son Jesus.

God's Greater Generosity

PSALM 23:5

> You prepare a table before me
> > in the presence of my enemies.
> You anoint my head with oil;
> > my cup overflows.

PROVERBS 11:24–25

> One person gives freely, yet gains even more;
> > another withholds unduly, but comes to poverty.
> A generous person will prosper;
> > whoever refreshes others will be refreshed.

MATTHEW 7:7–11

Ask and it will be given to you; seek and you will find; knock and the door will be opened to you. For everyone who asks receives; the one who seeks finds; and to the one who knocks, the door will be opened.

Which of you, if your son asks for bread, will give him a stone? Or if he asks for a fish, will give him a snake? If you, then, though you are evil, know how to give good gifts to your children, how much more will your Father in heaven give good gifts to those who ask him!

Lord, there have been generous people in my life, but you are more giving than anyone I know. Show me how to give as you give.

God's Generosity to the Poor

PSALM 68:9–10

You gave abundant showers, O God;
    you refreshed your weary inheritance.
Your people settled in it,
    and from your bounty, God, you provided for the poor.

LEVITICUS 25:35–36, 38

If any of your fellow Israelites become poor and are unable to support themselves among you, help them as you would a foreigner and stranger, so they can continue to live among you. Do not take interest or any profit from them, but fear your God, so that they may continue to live among you. . . . I am the LORD your God, who brought you out of Egypt to give you the land of Canaan and to be your God.

1 JOHN 3:16–18

This is how we know what love is: Jesus Christ laid down his life for us. And we ought to lay down our lives for our brothers and sisters. If anyone has material possessions and sees a brother or sister in need but has no pity on them, how can the love of God be in that person? Dear children, let us not love with words or speech but with actions and in truth.

~~~~~

God loves those who are poor and in need. Through His love, you can be generous with what you have.

Stewarding God's Generosity Well

PSALM 112:5

> Good will come to those who are generous and lend freely,
> who conduct their affairs with justice.

DEUTERONOMY 8:16–18

He gave you manna to eat in the wilderness, something your ancestors had never known, to humble and test you so that in the end it might go well with you. You may say to yourself, "My power and the strength of my hands have produced this wealth for me." But remember the LORD your God, for it is he who gives you the ability to produce wealth, and so confirms his covenant, which he swore to your ancestors, as it is today.

1 TIMOTHY 6:17–18

Command those who are rich in this present world not to be arrogant nor to put their hope in wealth, which is so uncertain, but to put their hope in God, who richly provides us with everything for our enjoyment. Command them to do good, to be rich in good deeds, and to be generous and willing to share.

When have you been blessed by the generosity of a fellow believer? How can you pass on the generosity of God to someone else today?

The Generosity of God's Commandments

PSALM 119:13–14

With my lips I recount
    all the laws that come from your mouth.
I rejoice in following your statutes
    as one rejoices in great riches.

ISAIAH 58:6–7

Is not this the kind of fasting I have chosen:
to loose the chains of injustice
    and untie the cords of the yoke,
to set the oppressed free
    and break every yoke?
Is it not to share your food with the hungry
    and to provide the poor wanderer with shelter—
when you see the naked, to clothe them,
    and not to turn away from your own flesh and blood?

MATTHEW 25:37–40

Then the righteous will answer him, "Lord, when did we see you hungry and feed you, or thirsty and give you something to drink? When did we see you a stranger and invite you in, or needing clothes and clothe you? When did we see you sick or in prison and go to visit you?"

The King will reply, "Truly I tell you, whatever you did for one of the least of these brothers and sisters of mine, you did for me."

Lord, you have generously revealed the way to live in right relationship with you and with others. Please teach me to be generous with you, with those around me, with your creation, and with myself.

God's Generous Provision

PSALM 104:14–16

He makes grass grow for the cattle,
  and plants for people to cultivate—
  bringing forth food from the earth:
wine that gladdens human hearts,
  oil to make their faces shine,
  and bread that sustains their hearts.
The trees of the LORD are well watered,
  the cedars of Lebanon that he planted.

EZEKIEL 47:12

Fruit trees of all kinds will grow on both banks of the river. Their leaves will not wither, nor will their fruit fail. Every month they will bear fruit, because the water from the sanctuary flows to them. Their fruit will serve for food and their leaves for healing.

MATTHEW 14:19–21

And he directed the people to sit down on the grass. Taking the five loaves and the two fish and looking up to heaven, he gave thanks and broke the loaves. Then he gave them to the disciples, and the disciples gave them to the people. They all ate and were satisfied, and the disciples picked up twelve basketfuls of broken pieces that were left over. The number of those who ate was about five thousand men, besides women and children.

God generally provides to sustain His beloved creation—even in ways you can't understand.

God's Generous Salvation

PSALM 65:4–5

Blessed are those you choose
and bring near to live in your courts!
We are filled with the good things of your house,
of your holy temple.
You answer us with awesome and righteous deeds,
God our Savior,
the hope of all the ends of the earth
and of the farthest seas.

JEREMIAH 33:6–7

I will heal my people and will let them enjoy abundant peace and security. I will bring Judah and Israel back from captivity and will rebuild them as they were before.

EPHESIANS 1:7–8

In him we have redemption through his blood, the forgiveness of sins, in accordance with the riches of God's grace that he lavished on us.

～～～

Where are you waiting for rescue or reconstruction in your life?
Ask God to show you the grace He has generously lavished on you,
and to strength your hope in His coming salvation.

God's Merciful Reply

PSALM 86:2–4

> You are my God; have mercy on me, Lord,
>> for I call to you all day long.
> Bring joy to your servant, Lord,
>> for I put my trust in you.

DANIEL 9:17–19

Now, our God, hear the prayers and petitions of your servant. For your sake, Lord, look with favor on your desolate sanctuary. Give ear, our God, and hear; open your eyes and see the desolation of the city that bears your Name. We do not make requests of you because we are righteous, but because of your great mercy. Lord, listen! Lord, forgive! Lord, hear and act! For your sake, my God, do not delay, because your city and your people bear your Name.

MATTHEW 20:30, 32–34

Two blind men were sitting by the roadside, and when they heard that Jesus was going by, they shouted, "Lord, Son of David, have mercy on us!" . . .

Jesus stopped and called them. "What do you want me to do for you?" he asked.

"Lord," they answered, "we want our sight."

Jesus had compassion on them and touched their eyes. Immediately they received their sight and followed him.

~~~~~~

Lord, I ask you for what I need, not because I am righteous but because of your great mercy. Lord Jesus Christ, Son of God, have mercy on me.

Waiting on God's Certain Compassion

PSALM 31:9–10

Be merciful to me, LORD, for I am in distress;
my eyes grow weak with sorrow,
my soul and body with grief.
My life is consumed by anguish
and my years by groaning;
my strength fails because of my affliction,
and my bones grow weak.

ISAIAH 30:18

Yet the LORD longs to be gracious to you;
therefore he will rise up to show you compassion.
For the LORD is a God of justice.
Blessed are all who wait for him!

JAMES 5:10–11

Brothers and sisters, as an example of patience in the face of suffering, take the prophets who spoke in the name of the Lord. As you know, we count as blessed those who have persevered. You have heard of Job's perseverance and have seen what the Lord finally brought about. The Lord is full of compassion and mercy.

Even amid suffering and anguish, you can wait on God's compassion and mercy with certainty.

God's Everlasting Generosity

PSALM 132:13–16

> For the LORD has chosen Zion,
>> he has desired it for his dwelling, saying,
> "This is my resting place for ever and ever;
>> here I will sit enthroned, for I have desired it.
> I will bless her with abundant provisions;
>> her poor I will satisfy with food.
> I will clothe her priests with salvation,
>> and her faithful people will ever sing for joy."

ISAIAH 55:6–7

> Seek the LORD while he may be found;
>> call on him while he is near.
> Let the wicked forsake their ways
>> and the unrighteous their thoughts.
> Let them turn to the LORD, and he will have mercy on them,
>> and to our God, for he will freely pardon.

TITUS 3:5–7

He saved us through the washing of rebirth and renewal by the Holy Spirit, whom he poured out on us generously through Jesus Christ our Savior, so that, having been justified by his grace, we might become heirs having the hope of eternal life.

~~~~~

How have you seen the Holy Spirit working to renew your life? Pray and thank God for pouring out His generosity on you—now and for eternity.

Faithful

Great is thy faithfulness, O God my Father,

there is no shadow of turning with thee.

Thou changest not, thy compassions, they fail not;

as thou hast been, thou forever wilt be.

Summer and winter and springtime and harvest,
sun, moon, and stars in their courses above
join with all nature in manifold witness
to thy great faithfulness, mercy, and love.

Pardon for sin and a peace that endureth,
thine own dear presence to cheer and to guide,
strength for today and bright hope for tomorrow,
blessings all mine, with ten thousand beside!

Great is thy faithfulness!
Great is thy faithfulness!
Morning by morning new mercies I see;
all I have needed thy hand hath provided.
Great is thy faithfulness, Lord, unto me!

Thomas O. Chisholm, 1923

The Faithfulness of Our God

PSALM 36:5–6

Your love, Lord, reaches to the heavens,
  your faithfulness to the skies.
Your righteousness is like the highest mountains,
  your justice like the great deep.

DEUTERONOMY 7:7–9

The Lord did not set his affection on you and choose you because
you were more numerous than other peoples, for you were the fewest of
all peoples. But it was because the Lord loved you and kept the oath
he swore to your ancestors that he brought you out with a mighty hand
and redeemed you from the land of slavery, from the power of Pharaoh
king of Egypt. Know therefore that the Lord your God is God; he is the
faithful God, keeping his covenant of love to a thousand generations of
those who love him and keep his commandments.

1 CORINTHIANS 1:7–9

Therefore you do not lack any spiritual gift as you eagerly wait for
our Lord Jesus Christ to be revealed. He will also keep you firm to the
end, so that you will be blameless on the day of our Lord Jesus Christ.
God is faithful, who has called you into fellowship with his Son, Jesus
Christ our Lord.

~~~~~

*Lord, thank you for always doing what you set out to do. Your
faithfulness stretches far beyond what I can see. I wait confidently
for when my fellowship with your Son, Jesus, is full and complete.*

God's Faithfulness to His Promises

PSALM 119:74–76

May those who fear you rejoice when they see me,
    for I have put my hope in your word.
I know, LORD, that your laws are righteous,
    and that in faithfulness you have afflicted me.
May your unfailing love be my comfort,
    according to your promise to your servant.

ZECHARIAH 8:7–8

This is what the LORD Almighty says: "I will save my people from the countries of the east and the west. I will bring them back to live in Jerusalem; they will be my people, and I will be faithful and righteous to them as their God."

1 THESSALONIANS 5:23–24

May God himself, the God of peace, sanctify you through and through. May your whole spirit, soul and body be kept blameless at the coming of our Lord Jesus Christ. The one who calls you is faithful, and he will do it.

~~~~~~

God will do everything He has promised to do.

God's Faithfulness
When We're Faithless

PSALM 89:30, 32–33

> If his sons forsake my law
> > and do not follow my statutes, . . .
> I will punish their sin with the rod,
> > their iniquity with flogging;
> but I will not take my love from him,
> > nor will I ever betray my faithfulness.

JEREMIAH 3:12–13

> "Return, faithless Israel," declares the Lord,
> > "I will frown on you no longer,
> for I am faithful," declares the Lord,
> > "I will not be angry forever.
> Only acknowledge your guilt."

2 TIMOTHY 2:11–13

> If we died with him,
> > we will also live with him;
> if we endure,
> > we will also reign with him.
> If we disown him,
> > he will also disown us;
> if we are faithless,
> > he remains faithful,
> > for he cannot disown himself.

~~~~~

Where have you been faithless to God recently? Acknowledge your sin, and thank Him for never betraying His faithfulness to you.

God's Faithfulness to the Nations

PSALM 98:2–3

> The LORD has made his salvation known
> and revealed his righteousness to the nations.
> He has remembered his love
> and his faithfulness to Israel;
> all the ends of the earth have seen
> the salvation of our God.

ISAIAH 55:3–5

> Give ear and come to me;
> listen, that you may live.
> I will make an everlasting covenant with you,
> my faithful love promised to David.
> See, I have made him a witness to the peoples,
> a ruler and commander of the peoples.
> Surely you will summon nations you know not,
> and nations you do not know will come running to you,
> because of the LORD your God,
> the Holy One of Israel,
> for he has endowed you with splendor.

REVELATION 1:4–5

> Grace and peace to you from him who is, and who was, and who
> is to come, and from the seven spirits before his throne, and from Jesus
> Christ, who is the faithful witness, the firstborn from the dead, and the
> ruler of the kings of the earth.

~~~

*Lord, thank you that you continue to draw those who don't know you
to yourself. Through my life, and through the lives of your people, please
make your faithfulness known to all the earth.*

God's Daily Faithfulness

PSALM 85:10–12

> Love and faithfulness meet together;
>> righteousness and peace kiss each other.
> Faithfulness springs forth from the earth,
>> and righteousness looks down from heaven.
> The LORD will indeed give what is good,
>> and our land will yield its harvest.

JOEL 2:23–24

> Be glad, people of Zion,
>> rejoice in the LORD your God,
> for he has given you the autumn rains
>> because he is faithful.
> He sends you abundant showers,
>> both autumn and spring rains, as before.
> The threshing floors will be filled with grain;
>> the vats will overflow with new wine and oil.

MATTHEW 6:26

Look at the birds of the air; they do not sow or reap or store away in barns, and yet your heavenly Father feeds them. Are you not much more valuable than they?

God sustains the world and its life-giving cycles because He is faithful to us every day.

God's Eternal Faithfulness

PSALM 89:1–4

> I will sing of the LORD's great love forever;
>> with my mouth I will make your faithfulness known
>> through all generations.
> I will declare that your love stands firm forever,
>> that you have established your faithfulness in heaven itself.
> You said, "I have made a covenant with my chosen one,
>> I have sworn to David my servant,
> 'I will establish your line forever
>> and make your throne firm through all generations.'"

HOSEA 2:19–20

> I will betroth you to me forever;
>> I will betroth you in righteousness and justice,
>> in love and compassion.
> I will betroth you in faithfulness,
>> and you will acknowledge the LORD.

HEBREWS 10:22–23

Let us draw near to God with a sincere heart and with the full assurance that faith brings, having our hearts sprinkled to cleanse us from a guilty conscience and having our bodies washed with pure water. Let us hold unswervingly to the hope we profess, for he who promised is faithful.

~~~~~

What do you feel when you pause to consider that God has promised to make you His forever? Pray and share your thoughts with Him.

Jesus, the Fullness of God's Faithfulness

PSALM 33:4

> The word of the LORD is right and true;
>> he is faithful in all he does.

ISAIAH 42:1–4

> Here is my servant, whom I uphold,
>> my chosen one in whom I delight;
> I will put my Spirit on him,
>> and he will bring justice to the nations.
> He will not shout or cry out,
>> or raise his voice in the streets.
> A bruised reed he will not break,
>> and a smoldering wick he will not snuff out.
> In faithfulness he will bring forth justice;
>> he will not falter or be discouraged
> till he establishes justice on earth.

2 CORINTHIANS 1:18–20

But as surely as God is faithful, our message to you is not "Yes" and "No." For the Son of God, Jesus Christ, who was preached among you by us—by me and Silas and Timothy—was not "Yes" and "No," but in him it has always been "Yes." For no matter how many promises God has made, they are "Yes" in Christ. And so through him the "Amen" is spoken by us to the glory of God.

~~~

Lord, all your promises to bring rightness and justice and truth to your world find their "Yes" in Jesus. Thank you for making restoration possible after promising that you would.

God's Faithful Jealousy

PSALM 78:56–58

> But they put God to the test
> and rebelled against the Most High;
> they did not keep his statutes.
> Like their ancestors they were disloyal and faithless,
> as unreliable as a faulty bow.
> They angered him with their high places;
> they aroused his jealousy with their idols.

EXODUS 34:14–15

Do not worship any other god, for the LORD, whose name is Jealous, is a jealous God.

Be careful not to make a treaty with those who live in the land; for when they prostitute themselves to their gods and sacrifice to them, they will invite you and you will eat their sacrifices.

ROMANS 12:1–2

Therefore, I urge you, brothers and sisters, in view of God's mercy, to offer your bodies as a living sacrifice, holy and pleasing to God—this is your true and proper worship. Do not conform to the pattern of this world, but be transformed by the renewing of your mind.

~~~~~

God is jealous of your worship, love, and fidelity because they rightly belong to Him.

God's Burning Jealousy

PSALM 50:3–5

Our God comes
    and will not be silent;
a fire devours before him,
    and around him a tempest rages.
He summons the heavens above,
    and the earth, that he may judge his people:
"Gather to me this consecrated people,
    who made a covenant with me by sacrifice."

DEUTERONOMY 4:23–24

Be careful not to forget the covenant of the LORD your God that he made with you; do not make for yourselves an idol in the form of anything the LORD your God has forbidden. For the LORD your God is a consuming fire, a jealous God.

HEBREWS 12:28–29

Therefore, since we are receiving a kingdom that cannot be shaken, let us be thankful, and so worship God acceptably with reverence and awe, for our "God is a consuming fire."

Is there an area of your life where you are being unfaithful to God? Confess to Him, and ask Him to burn up your unfaithfulness in the fire of His jealousy.

God's Jealousy for His People

PSALM 135:3–4

Praise the LORD, for the LORD is good;
  sing praise to his name, for that is pleasant.
For the LORD has chosen Jacob to be his own,
  Israel to be his treasured possession.

ZECHARIAH 8:2–3

This is what the LORD Almighty says: "I am very jealous for Zion; I am burning with jealousy for her."

This is what the LORD says: "I will return to Zion and dwell in Jerusalem. Then Jerusalem will be called the Faithful City, and the mountain of the LORD Almighty will be called the Holy Mountain."

1 CORINTHIANS 6:19–20

Do you not know that your bodies are temples of the Holy Spirit, who is in you, whom you have received from God? You are not your own; you were bought at a price. Therefore honor God with your bodies.

~~~~~

Lord, thank you for treasuring your people and putting your Spirit inside of me. When I forget, remind me that you are jealous of me because you love me and have made me your own.

God's Reconciling Jealousy

PSALM 79:3–5

> They have poured out blood like water
> all around Jerusalem,
> and there is no one to bury the dead.
> We are objects of contempt to our neighbors,
> of scorn and derision to those around us.
>
> How long, Lord? Will you be angry forever?
> How long will your jealousy burn like fire?

JOEL 2:18–19

> Then the Lord was jealous for his land
> and took pity on his people.

The Lord replied to them:

> "I am sending you grain, new wine and olive oil,
> enough to satisfy you fully;
> never again will I make you
> an object of scorn to the nations."

JAMES 4:4–6

You adulterous people, don't you know that friendship with the world means enmity against God? Therefore, anyone who chooses to be a friend of the world becomes an enemy of God. Or do you think Scripture says without reason that he jealously longs for the spirit he has caused to dwell in us? But he gives us more grace.

~~~

The pain, brokenness, and sin of the world all point you back to God, who longs to reconcile you to himself.

The Strength of God's Jealousy

PSALM 89:46–49

How long, Lord? Will you hide yourself forever?
How long will your wrath burn like fire?
Remember how fleeting is my life.
For what futility you have created all humanity!
Who can live and not see death,
or who can escape the power of the grave?
Lord, where is your former great love,
which in your faithfulness you swore to David?

SONG OF SONGS 8:6

Place me like a seal over your heart,
like a seal on your arm;
for love is as strong as death,
its jealousy unyielding as the grave.
It burns like blazing fire,
like a mighty flame.

JOHN 2:13–17

When it was almost time for the Jewish Passover, Jesus went up to Jerusalem. In the temple courts he found people selling cattle, sheep and doves, and others sitting at tables exchanging money. So he made a whip out of cords, and drove all from the temple courts, both sheep and cattle; he scattered the coins of the money changers and overturned their tables. To those who sold doves he said, "Get these out of here! Stop turning my Father's house into a market!" His disciples remembered that it is written: "Zeal for your house will consume me."

What word or phrase from the passages above stood out to you?
Pause to talk with God about it.

God's Jealousy Tolerates No Rivals

PSALM 86:11

Teach me your way, Lord,
    that I may rely on your faithfulness;
give me an undivided heart,
    that I may fear your name.

ZEPHANIAH 1:18

"Neither their silver nor their gold
    will be able to save them
    on the day of the Lord's wrath."

In the fire of his jealousy
    the whole earth will be consumed,
for he will make a sudden end
    of all who live on the earth.

MATTHEW 6:24

No one can serve two masters. Either you will hate the one and love the other, or you will be devoted to the one and despise the other. You cannot serve both God and money.

~~~~~~

Lord, I'm sorry that sometimes I worship other things and think they deserve the devotion and power I give to them. I want your faithful jealousy to bring me back to you.

God's Jealousy for True Worship

PSALM 145:17–18

The LORD is righteous in all his ways
    and faithful in all he does.
The LORD is near to all who call on him,
    to all who call on him in truth.

DEUTERONOMY 32:16–18

They made him jealous with their foreign gods
    and angered him with their detestable idols.
They sacrificed to false gods, which are not God—
    gods they had not known,
    gods that recently appeared,
    gods your ancestors did not fear.
You deserted the Rock, who fathered you;
    you forgot the God who gave you birth.

2 CORINTHIANS 11:2–4

I am jealous for you with a godly jealousy. I promised you to one husband, to Christ. . . . But I am afraid . . . your minds may somehow be led astray from your sincere and pure devotion to Christ. For if someone comes to you and preaches a Jesus other than the Jesus we preached, or if you receive a different spirit from the Spirit you received, or a different gospel from the one you accepted, you put up with it easily enough.

God wants you to know who He truly is, so you can worship Him for who He truly is.

God's Faithful Forgiveness

PSALM 103:12

> As far as the east is from the west,
>> so far has he removed our transgressions from us.

JEREMIAH 31:33–34

> I will put my law in their minds
>> and write it on their hearts.
> I will be their God,
>> and they will be my people. . . .
> For I will forgive their wickedness
>> and will remember their sins no more.

HEBREWS 10:15–18

> The Holy Spirit also testifies to us about this. First he says:

> "This is the covenant I will make with them
>> after that time, says the Lord.
> I will put my laws in their hearts,
>> and I will write them on their minds."

Then he adds:

> "Their sins and lawless acts
>> I will remember no more."

And where these have been forgiven, sacrifice for sin is no longer necessary.

What do you need to ask God's forgiveness for today? Talk with Him about it, and thank Him for already being ready to forgive you.

God's Cleansing Forgiveness

PSALM 51:7–9

Cleanse me with hyssop, and I will be clean;
    wash me, and I will be whiter than snow.
Let me hear joy and gladness;
    let the bones you have crushed rejoice.
Hide your face from my sins
    and blot out all my iniquity.

ISAIAH 1:18–20

"Come now, let us settle the matter,"
    says the LORD.
"Though your sins are like scarlet,
    they shall be as white as snow;
though they are red as crimson,
    they shall be like wool.
If you are willing and obedient,
    you will eat the good things of the land;
but if you resist and rebel,
    you will be devoured by the sword."
For the mouth of the LORD has spoken.

1 JOHN 1:8–9

If we claim to be without sin, we deceive ourselves and the truth is not in us. If we confess our sins, he is faithful and just and will forgive us our sins and purify us from all unrighteousness.

~~~

Lord, I feel marked by the sin, failure, and brokenness in my life. Thank you that you are faithful to cleanse me, purifying me from wrongdoing against you and against others.

God's Undeserved Forgiveness

PSALM 32:1–2

Blessed is the one
whose transgressions are forgiven,
whose sins are covered.
Blessed is the one
whose sin the LORD does not count against them
and in whose spirit is no deceit.

DANIEL 9:9–11

The Lord our God is merciful and forgiving, even though we have rebelled against him; we have not obeyed the LORD our God or kept the laws he gave us through his servants the prophets. All Israel has transgressed your law and turned away, refusing to obey you.

COLOSSIANS 2:13–14

When you were dead in your sins and in the uncircumcision of your flesh, God made you alive with Christ. He forgave us all our sins, having canceled the charge of our legal indebtedness, which stood against us and condemned us; he has taken it away, nailing it to the cross.

~~~~~

God forgives us, not because we deserve it but because He's merciful and faithful. It's who He is.

God's Just Forgiveness

PSALM 32:5–6

Then I acknowledged my sin to you
    and did not cover up my iniquity.
I said, "I will confess
    my transgressions to the LORD."
And you forgave
    the guilt of my sin.

Therefore let all the faithful pray to you
    while you may be found.

MALACHI 3:17–18

"On the day when I act," says the LORD Almighty, "they will be
my treasured possession. I will spare them, just as a father has compassion
and spares his son who serves him. And you will again see the distinction
between the righteous and the wicked, between those who serve God and
those who do not."

MATTHEW 6:12–15

Forgive us our debts,
    as we also have forgiven our debtors.
And lead us not into temptation
    but deliver us from the evil one.

For if you forgive other people when they sin against you, your heavenly
Father will also forgive you. But if you do not forgive others their sins,
your Father will not forgive your sins.

~~~~~~

*When have you forgiven someone else, or asked someone else for
forgiveness? Ask God to help you grow in both offering and
receiving forgiveness.*

God's Forgiveness for His Sake

PSALM 79:8–10

> Do not hold against us the sins of past generations;
>> may your mercy come quickly to meet us,
>> for we are in desperate need.
> Help us, God our Savior,
>> for the glory of your name;
> deliver us and forgive our sins
>> for your name's sake.
> Why should the nations say,
>> "Where is their God?"

ISAIAH 43:24–25

> You have burdened me with your sins
>> and wearied me with your offenses.
> I, even I, am he who blots out
>> your transgressions, for my own sake,
>> and remembers your sins no more.

ACTS 10:41–43

[Jesus] was not seen by all the people, but by witnesses whom God had already chosen—by us who ate and drank with him after he rose from the dead. He commanded us to preach to the people and to testify that he is the one whom God appointed as judge of the living and the dead. All the prophets testify about him that everyone who believes in him receives forgiveness of sins through his name.

~~~~~~

Lord, I often forget that you forgive me not just for my sake but also for your sake. I'm so thankful you want to be in a loving relationship with me. Help me to value our relationship as much as you do.

God's Forgiving Response to Repentance

PSALM 86:5

You, Lord, are forgiving and good,
    abounding in love to all who call to you.

2 CHRONICLES 7:13–15

When I shut up the heavens so that there is no rain, or command locusts to devour the land or send a plague among my people, if my people, who are called by my name, will humble themselves and pray and seek my face and turn from their wicked ways, then I will hear from heaven, and I will forgive their sin and will heal their land. Now my eyes will be open and my ears attentive to the prayers offered in this place.

LUKE 24:45–47

Then [Jesus] opened their minds so they could understand the Scriptures. He told them, "This is what is written: The Messiah will suffer and rise from the dead on the third day, and repentance for the forgiveness of sins will be preached in his name to all nations, beginning at Jerusalem."

~~~~~

God is faithful to forgive you when you repent of your sins and turn to Him.

With God There Is Forgiveness

PSALM 130:3–4

If you, LORD, kept a record of sins,
Lord, who could stand?
But with you there is forgiveness,
so that we can, with reverence, serve you.

JOEL 2:13–14

Rend your heart
and not your garments.
Return to the LORD your God,
for he is gracious and compassionate,
slow to anger and abounding in love,
and he relents from sending calamity.
Who knows? He may turn and relent
and leave behind a blessing—
grain offerings and drink offerings
for the LORD your God.

LUKE 23:32–34

Two other men, both criminals, were also led out with him to be executed. When they came to the place called the Skull, they crucified him there, along with the criminals—one on his right, the other on his left. Jesus said, "Father, forgive them, for they do not know what they are doing."

～～

Are you keeping a record of your own sins or someone else's sins?
Ask God to remind you of His faithful forgiveness and restoration.

God's Immense Patience

PSALM 90:4

A thousand years in your sight
   are like a day that has just gone by,
   or like a watch in the night.

NEHEMIAH 9:30–31

For many years you were patient with them. By your Spirit you
warned them through your prophets. Yet they paid no attention, so you
gave them into the hands of the neighboring peoples. But in your great
mercy you did not put an end to them or abandon them, for you are a
gracious and merciful God.

1 TIMOTHY 1:15–17

Here is a trustworthy saying that deserves full acceptance: Christ
Jesus came into the world to save sinners—of whom I am the worst.
But for that very reason I was shown mercy so that in me, the worst of
sinners, Christ Jesus might display his immense patience as an example
for those who would believe in him and receive eternal life. Now to the
King eternal, immortal, invisible, the only God, be honor and glory for
ever and ever. Amen.

~~~~~

*Lord, you are more patient than anyone I know. In your immense
patience, you show me your mercy, grace, and faithfulness. Teach me
to be patient like you.*

God's Patience with Our Sin

PSALM 40:11–13

Do not withhold your mercy from me, LORD;
    may your love and faithfulness always protect me.
For troubles without number surround me;
    my sins have overtaken me, and I cannot see.
They are more than the hairs of my head,
    and my heart fails within me.
Be pleased to save me, LORD;
    come quickly, LORD, to help me.

EZEKIEL 20:21–22

But the children rebelled against me: They did not follow my decrees, they were not careful to keep my laws. . . . So I said I would pour out my wrath on them and spend my anger against them in the wilderness. But I withheld my hand, and for the sake of my name I did what would keep it from being profaned in the eyes of the nations in whose sight I had brought them out.

ROMANS 3:25

God presented Christ as a sacrifice of atonement, through the shedding of his blood—to be received by faith. He did this to demonstrate his righteousness, because in his forbearance he had left the sins committed beforehand unpunished.

~~~~

God is patient with your sin so He can faithfully reconcile you to himself through Christ.

The Long-Suffering of Christ

PSALM 34:19–20

The righteous person may have many troubles,
 but the LORD delivers him from them all;
he protects all his bones,
 not one of them will be broken.*

ISAIAH 53:1–3

Who has believed our message
 and to whom has the arm of the LORD been revealed?
He grew up before him like a tender shoot,
 and like a root out of dry ground.
He had no beauty or majesty to attract us to him,
 nothing in his appearance that we should desire him.
He was despised and rejected by mankind,
 a man of suffering, and familiar with pain.

1 PETER 2:21–23

Christ suffered for you, leaving you an example, that you should follow in his steps.

"He committed no sin,
 and no deceit was found in his mouth."

When they hurled their insults at him, he did not retaliate; when he suffered, he made no threats. Instead, he entrusted himself to him who judges justly.

~~~

What do you feel when you stop to think about how Christ patiently suffered for you? Talk with God, thanking Him for His faithfulness to you.

---

* This messianic psalm was fulfilled at Jesus's crucifixion. Roman soldiers broke victims' legs to hasten death, but the Roman soldiers did not break Jesus's legs because He had already died (John 19:31–37).

God's Inscrutable Patience

PSALM 73:12–14

This is what the wicked are like—
    always free of care, they go on amassing wealth.
Surely in vain I have kept my heart pure
    and have washed my hands in innocence.
All day long I have been afflicted,
    and every morning brings new punishments.

ECCLESIASTES 8:11–13

When the sentence for a crime is not quickly carried out, people's hearts are filled with schemes to do wrong. Although a wicked person who commits a hundred crimes may live a long time, I know that it will go better with those who fear God, who are reverent before him. Yet because the wicked do not fear God, it will not go well with them, and their days will not lengthen like a shadow.

ROMANS 9:22–23

What if God, although choosing to show his wrath and make his power known, bore with great patience the objects of his wrath—prepared for destruction? What if he did this to make the riches of his glory known to the objects of his mercy, whom he prepared in advance for glory?

~~~~~

Lord, I don't fully understand your patience with evil, when people knowingly harm each other, themselves, and your creation. Please help me to trust your faithfulness even when I don't get it.

God's Patience Requires the Patience of His People

PSALM 40:1–2

I waited patiently for the LORD;
  he turned to me and heard my cry.
He lifted me out of the slimy pit,
  out of the mud and mire;
he set my feet on a rock
  and gave me a firm place to stand.

LAMENTATIONS 3:25–27

The LORD is good to those whose hope is in him,
  to the one who seeks him;
it is good to wait quietly
  for the salvation of the LORD.
It is good for a man to bear the yoke
  while he is young.

1 PETER 5:10–11

And the God of all grace, who called you to his eternal glory in Christ, after you have suffered a little while, will himself restore you and make you strong, firm and steadfast. To him be the power for ever and ever. Amen.

~~~~~

Because God is patient with His creation, you have to learn to go at His pace too.

God's Patience Means Salvation

PSALM 75:2–3

> You say, "I choose the appointed time;
> it is I who judge with equity.
> When the earth and all its people quake,
> it is I who hold its pillars firm."

JONAH 3:1–5

Then the word of the LORD came to Jonah a second time: "Go to the great city of Nineveh and proclaim to it the message I give you."

Jonah obeyed the word of the LORD and went to Nineveh. Now Nineveh was a very large city; it took three days to go through it. Jonah began by going a day's journey into the city, proclaiming, "Forty more days and Nineveh will be overthrown." The Ninevites believed God. A fast was proclaimed, and all of them, from the greatest to the least, put on sackcloth.

2 PETER 3:14–16

Make every effort to be found spotless, blameless and at peace with him. Bear in mind that our Lord's patience means salvation, just as our dear brother Paul also wrote you with the wisdom that God gave him. He writes the same way in all his letters, speaking in them of these matters.

~~~

Where in your life are you feeling impatient with God's timing? What might God be patiently doing in this time that feels wasted to you?

Our Certainty in God's Patience

PSALM 27:13–14

> I remain confident of this:
>> I will see the goodness of the LORD
>> in the land of the living.
> Wait for the LORD;
>> be strong and take heart
>> and wait for the LORD.

HABAKKUK 2:3

> The revelation awaits an appointed time;
>> it speaks of the end
>> and will not prove false.
> Though it linger, wait for it;
>> it will certainly come
>> and will not delay.

HEBREWS 10:36–37

You need to persevere so that when you have done the will of God, you will receive what he has promised. For,

> "In just a little while,
>> he who is coming will come
>> and will not delay."

Lord, I'm waiting for so many things I'm not sure about. Remind me that I can wait confidently for you. I am certain you are coming.

God's Faithfulness to All Generations

PSALM 100:4–5

> Enter his gates with thanksgiving
> > and his courts with praise;
> > give thanks to him and praise his name.
> For the LORD is good and his love endures forever;
> > his faithfulness continues through all generations.

ISAIAH 61:8–9

> In my faithfulness I will reward my people
> > and make an everlasting covenant with them.
> Their descendants will be known among the nations
> > and their offspring among the peoples.
> All who see them will acknowledge
> > that they are a people the LORD has blessed.

ROMANS 3:3–5

What if some were unfaithful? Will their unfaithfulness nullify God's faithfulness? Not at all! Let God be true, and every human being a liar. As it is written:

> "So that you may be proved right when you speak
> > and prevail when you judge."

But if our unrighteousness brings out God's righteousness more clearly, what shall we say?

~~~~~~

God was faithful in the past, He is faithful in the present, and He will be faithful in the future.

Our Faithful, Forgiving God

PSALM 25:10–11

> All the ways of the LORD are loving and faithful
>> toward those who keep the demands of his covenant.
> For the sake of your name, LORD,
>> forgive my iniquity, though it is great.

PROVERBS 19:11

> A person's wisdom yields patience;
>> it is to one's glory to overlook an offense.

COLOSSIANS 3:12–14

Therefore, as God's chosen people, holy and dearly loved, clothe yourselves with compassion, kindness, humility, gentleness and patience. Bear with each other and forgive one another if any of you has a grievance against someone. Forgive as the Lord forgave you. And over all these virtues put on love, which binds them all together in perfect unity.

~~~~~~

What is something you're grateful God has forgiven you for? Pray and ask Him to clothe you with His compassion, kindness, humility, gentleness, and patience, so you can forgive as He forgives.

Transcendent

O pow'r of love, all else transcending,

in Jesus present evermore,

I worship thee, in homage bending,

and sing of thy celestial lore:

yea, let my soul, in deep devotion,

bathe in love's mighty boundless ocean.

Thou art my rest, no earthly treasure
can satisfy my yearning heart,
and naught can give to me the pleasure
I find in thee, my chosen part.
Thy love, so tender and caressing,
is joy to me, and every blessing.

To thee my heart and life be given,
thou art in truth my highest Good;
for me thy sacred side was riven,
for me was shed thy precious blood.
O thou who art the world's salvation,
be thine my love and adoration.

Gerhard Tersteegen, 1700s
translated from German by Herman Brueckner

God's Complete Transcendence

PSALM 8:3–4

When I consider your heavens,
the work of your fingers,
the moon and the stars,
which you have set in place,
what is mankind that you are mindful of them,
human beings that you care for them?

ISAIAH 55:8–9

"For my thoughts are not your thoughts,
neither are your ways my ways,"
declares the LORD.
"As the heavens are higher than the earth,
so are my ways higher than your ways
and my thoughts than your thoughts."

PHILIPPIANS 2:9–11

Therefore God exalted him to the highest place
and gave him the name that is above every name,
that at the name of Jesus every knee should bow,
in heaven and on earth and under the earth,
and every tongue acknowledge that Jesus Christ is Lord,
to the glory of God the Father.

~~~

*Lord, your power, creativity, and thinking are so far above mine,
I can't fully comprehend you. I feel small in a good way. Thank you
for caring for me and loving me all the same.*

God Transcends All Creation

PSALM 108:3–5

I will praise you, LORD, among the nations;
    I will sing of you among the peoples.
For great is your love, higher than the heavens;
    your faithfulness reaches to the skies.
Be exalted, O God, above the heavens;
    let your glory be over all the earth.

1 KINGS 8:27–28

But will God really dwell on earth? The heavens, even the highest heaven, cannot contain you. How much less this temple I have built! Yet give attention to your servant's prayer and his plea for mercy, LORD my God. Hear the cry and the prayer that your servant is praying in your presence this day.

ACTS 7:48–50

However, the Most High does not live in houses made by human hands. As the prophet says:

"Heaven is my throne,
    and the earth is my footstool.
What kind of house will you build for me?
says the Lord.
    Or where will my resting place be?
Has not my hand made all these things?"

As complex and overwhelming as creation is, it cannot contain or compare with God.

God's Rule Transcends All Authority

PSALM 47:2–4

For the LORD Most High is awesome,
    the great King over all the earth.
He subdued nations under us,
    peoples under our feet.
He chose our inheritance for us,
    the pride of Jacob, whom he loved.

ISAIAH 40:21–22

Do you not know?
    Have you not heard?
Has it not been told you from the beginning?
    Have you not understood since the earth was founded?
He sits enthroned above the circle of the earth,
    and its people are like grasshoppers.
He stretches out the heavens like a canopy,
    and spreads them out like a tent to live in.

EPHESIANS 1:18–21

I pray that . . . you may know the hope to which he has called you, the riches of his glorious inheritance in his holy people, and his incomparably great power for us who believe. That power is the same as the mighty strength he exerted when he raised Christ from the dead and seated him at his right hand in the heavenly realms, far above all rule and authority, power and dominion, and every name that is invoked, not only in the present age but also in the one to come.

Where do you see authority misused in the world? Talk with God about it, and thank Him that true authority rests with His Son, Jesus Christ.

God Transcends All Other "Gods"

PSALM 96:4–6

> For great is the LORD and most worthy of praise;
> > he is to be feared above all gods.
> For all the gods of the nations are idols,
> > but the LORD made the heavens.
> Splendor and majesty are before him;
> > strength and glory are in his sanctuary.

JEREMIAH 10:14–16

> Everyone is senseless and without knowledge;
> > every goldsmith is shamed by his idols.
> The images he makes are a fraud;
> > they have no breath in them.
> They are worthless, the objects of mockery;
> > when their judgment comes, they will perish.
> He who is the Portion of Jacob is not like these,
> > for he is the Maker of all things,
> including Israel, the people of his inheritance—
> > the LORD Almighty is his name.

ACTS 17:29–30

Therefore since we are God's offspring, we should not think that the divine being is like gold or silver or stone—an image made by human design and skill. In the past God overlooked such ignorance, but now he commands all people everywhere to repent.

~~~~

Lord, too often I want to be able to contain you and put you in a box that I understand. Forgive me. When I need it, please remind me that you are so much greater than I know.

God Transcends All Human Wisdom

PSALM 97:8–9

Zion hears and rejoices
     and the villages of Judah are glad
     because of your judgments, LORD.
For you, LORD, are the Most High over all the earth.

ECCLESIASTES 5:1–2

Guard your steps when you go to the house of God. Go near to listen rather than to offer the sacrifice of fools, who do not know that they do wrong.

Do not be quick with your mouth,
     do not be hasty in your heart
     to utter anything before God.
God is in heaven
     and you are on earth,
     so let your words be few.

1 CORINTHIANS 1:25

For the foolishness of God is wiser than human wisdom, and the weakness of God is stronger than human strength.

God's infinite wisdom invites us to listen and learn from Him.

God Transcends Heaven and Earth

PSALM 8:1

Lord, our Lord,
how majestic is your name in all the earth!

You have set your glory
in the heavens.

DEUTERONOMY 4:39

Acknowledge and take to heart this day that the Lord is God in heaven above and on the earth below. There is no other.

JOHN 8:21–23

Once more Jesus said to them, "I am going away, and you will look for me, and you will die in your sin. Where I go, you cannot come."

This made the Jews ask, "Will he kill himself? Is that why he says, 'Where I go, you cannot come'?"

But he continued, "You are from below; I am from above. You are of this world; I am not of this world."

~~~~~

What is one area of life where you are glad God transcends human perspectives and concerns? Thank Him for being so far above His creation.

God Transcends Everything Seen and Unseen

PSALM 47:5–7

God has ascended amid shouts of joy,
the LORD amid the sounding of trumpets.
Sing praises to God, sing praises;
sing praises to our King, sing praises.
For God is the King of all the earth;
sing to him a psalm of praise.

JOB 26:5–8

The dead are in deep anguish,
those beneath the waters and all that live in them.
The realm of the dead is naked before God;
Destruction lies uncovered.
He spreads out the northern skies over empty space;
he suspends the earth over nothing.
He wraps up the waters in his clouds,
yet the clouds do not burst under their weight.

HEBREWS 11:3

By faith we understand that the universe was formed at God's command, so that what is seen was not made out of what was visible.

Lord, the world I can taste and touch is already too big for me to wrap my mind around. There's even more to reality that I can't see or perceive. Thank you for being King over it all.

Our Infinite God

PSALM 145:3–5

> Great is the LORD and most worthy of praise;
>> his greatness no one can fathom.
> One generation commends your works to another;
>> they tell of your mighty acts.
> They speak of the glorious splendor of your majesty—
>> and I will meditate on your wonderful works.

JOB 42:1–3

> Then Job replied to the LORD:

> "I know that you can do all things;
>> no purpose of yours can be thwarted.
> You asked, 'Who is this that obscures my plans without knowledge?'
>> Surely I spoke of things I did not understand,
>> things too wonderful for me to know."

EPHESIANS 3:20–21

Now to him who is able to do immeasurably more than all we ask or imagine, according to his power that is at work within us, to him be glory in the church and in Christ Jesus throughout all generations, for ever and ever! Amen.

~~~~

God's power, splendor, and knowledge are infinite—far beyond what we can ask or imagine.

God's Infinity and Our Finitude

PSALM 144:3–5, 7

> LORD, what are human beings that you care for them,
>> mere mortals that you think of them?
> They are like a breath;
>> their days are like a fleeting shadow.
>
> Part your heavens, LORD, and come down. . . .
> Reach down your hand from on high;
>> deliver me and rescue me
> from the mighty waters.

ISAIAH 40:15–17

> Surely the nations are like a drop in a bucket;
>> they are regarded as dust on the scales;
>> he weighs the islands as though they were fine dust.
> Lebanon is not sufficient for altar fires,
>> nor its animals enough for burnt offerings.
> Before him all the nations are as nothing;
>> they are regarded by him as worthless
>> and less than nothing.

MATTHEW 19:26

Jesus looked at them and said, "With man this is impossible, but with God all things are possible."

~~~~

When have you doubted God's ability or decision-making? Ask God to remind you of who He is.

God's Infinite Knowledge

PSALM 38:9–10

> All my longings lie open before you, Lord;
>> my sighing is not hidden from you.
> My heart pounds, my strength fails me;
>> even the light has gone from my eyes.

1 CHRONICLES 28:9

And you, my son Solomon, acknowledge the God of your father, and serve him with wholehearted devotion and with a willing mind, for the LORD searches every heart and understands every desire and every thought.

EPHESIANS 1:22–23

And God placed all things under his feet and appointed him to be head over everything for the church, which is his body, the fullness of him who fills everything in every way.

~~~~~

Lord, you know everything: every thought, every sigh, every desire. When I'm worried about what I don't know, help me to rest in your knowledge.

God's Infinite Reign

PSALM 146:10

The Lord reigns forever,
your God, O Zion, for all generations.

2 KINGS 19:14–16

Hezekiah received the letter from the messengers and read it.
Then he went up to the temple of the LORD and spread it out before
the LORD. And Hezekiah prayed to the LORD: "LORD, the God of
Israel, enthroned between the cherubim, you alone are God over all
the kingdoms of the earth. You have made heaven and earth. Give ear,
LORD, and hear; open your eyes, LORD, and see."

REVELATION 11:15

The seventh angel sounded his trumpet, and there were loud
voices in heaven, which said:

"The kingdom of the world has become
the kingdom of our Lord and of his Messiah,
and he will reign for ever and ever."

~~~~~~

*God is bringing His kingdom to earth, to rule completely over
all creation.*

God's Infinite Discernment

PSALM 53:2

> God looks down from heaven
>> on all mankind
> to see if there are any who understand,
>> any who seek God.

AMOS 9:2–3

> Though they dig down to the depths below,
>> from there my hand will take them.
> Though they climb up to the heavens above,
>> from there I will bring them down.
> Though they hide themselves on the top of Carmel,
>> there I will hunt them down and seize them.
> Though they hide from my eyes at the bottom of the sea,
>> there I will command the serpent to bite them.

REVELATION 22:12–13

Look, I am coming soon! My reward is with me, and I will give to each person according to what they have done. I am the Alpha and the Omega, the First and the Last, the Beginning and the End.

~~~~~

What word or phrase from the passages above stood out to you? Pause to talk with God about it.

God's Infinite Care

PSALM 118:6–7

> The LORD is with me; I will not be afraid.
> > What can mere mortals do to me?
> The LORD is with me; he is my helper.
> > I look in triumph on my enemies.

2 CHRONICLES 20:6

LORD, the God of our ancestors, are you not the God who is in heaven? You rule over all the kingdoms of the nations. Power and might are in your hand, and no one can withstand you.

HEBREWS 13:5–6

Keep your lives free from the love of money and be content with what you have, because God has said,

> "Never will I leave you;
> > never will I forsake you."

So we say with confidence,

> "The Lord is my helper; I will not be afraid.
> > What can mere mortals do to me?"

Lord, you never leave me or forsake me. When I feel alone or unseen, please reveal your presence to me. I want to say with confidence, "You are my helper. I will not be afraid."

God's Infinite Ability

PSALM 115:15–16

> May you be blessed by the Lord,
>> the Maker of heaven and earth.

> The highest heavens belong to the Lord.

JEREMIAH 32:17–19

Ah, Sovereign Lord, you have made the heavens and the earth by your great power and outstretched arm. Nothing is too hard for you. You show love to thousands but bring the punishment for the parents' sins into the laps of their children after them. Great and mighty God, whose name is the Lord Almighty, great are your purposes and mighty are your deeds. Your eyes are open to the ways of all mankind; you reward each person according to their conduct and as their deeds deserve.

LUKE 1:37

No word from God will ever fail.

~~~~~~

God created and sustains everything around you. Nothing is too hard for Him.

Our Eternal God

PSALM 9:7–8

> The LORD reigns forever;
>> he has established his throne for judgment.
> He rules the world in righteousness
>> and judges the peoples with equity.

DEUTERONOMY 33:26–27

> There is no one like the God of Jeshurun,
>> who rides across the heavens to help you
>> and on the clouds in his majesty.
> The eternal God is your refuge,
>> and underneath are the everlasting arms.

ROMANS 1:19–20

What may be known about God is plain to them, because God has made it plain to them. For since the creation of the world God's invisible qualities—his eternal power and divine nature—have been clearly seen, being understood from what has been made, so that people are without excuse.

〜〜

Where are you feeling limited by your age or time? Ask God to meet you in your limitations and help you know that His everlasting arms are under you.

God's Eternal Kingdom

PSALM 45:6

Your throne, O God, will last for ever and ever;
a scepter of justice will be the scepter of your kingdom.

EXODUS 15:17–18

You will bring them in and plant them
on the mountain of your inheritance—
the place, Lord, you made for your dwelling,
the sanctuary, Lord, your hands established.

"The Lord reigns
for ever and ever."

REVELATION 4:9–10

Whenever the living creatures give glory, honor and thanks to him who sits on the throne and who lives for ever and ever, the twenty-four elders fall down before him who sits on the throne and worship him who lives for ever and ever. They lay their crowns before the throne.

Lord, governments and leaders come and go, but you reign for ever and ever. Thank you that yours is a kingdom of justice, community, and gratitude.

God's Offer of Eternity
to Frail Humanity

PSALM 39:4–5

Show me, LORD, my life's end
　　and the number of my days;
　　let me know how fleeting my life is.
You have made my days a mere handbreadth;
　　the span of my years is as nothing before you.
Everyone is but a breath,
　　even those who seem secure.

ISAIAH 40:6–8

All people are like grass,
　　and all their faithfulness is like the flowers of the field.
The grass withers and the flowers fall,
　　because the breath of the LORD blows on them.
　　Surely the people are grass.
The grass withers and the flowers fall,
　　but the word of our God endures forever.

ROMANS 6:22–23

But now that you have been set free from sin and have become
slaves of God, the benefit you reap leads to holiness, and the result is
eternal life. For the wages of sin is death, but the gift of God is eternal
life in Christ Jesus our Lord.

～

*God offers you His eternal life and holiness through the gift of
His Son, Jesus.*

Our Eternal Praise
to Our Eternal God

PSALM 145:1–2

I will exalt you, my God the King;
   I will praise your name for ever and ever.
Every day I will praise you
   and extol your name for ever and ever.

ECCLESIASTES 3:10–11

I have seen the burden God has laid on the human race. He has
made everything beautiful in its time. He has also set eternity in the
human heart; yet no one can fathom what God has done from beginning
to end.

EPHESIANS 1:4–6

He chose us in him before the creation of the world to be holy and
blameless in his sight. In love he predestined us for adoption to sonship
through Jesus Christ, in accordance with his pleasure and will—to the
praise of his glorious grace, which he has freely given us in the One he
loves.

*What can you praise God for today? Tell Him now, and thank Him
that because of His glorious grace, you will always have something to
praise Him for—for the rest of eternity.*

Our God from Eternity Past

PSALM 41:12–13

Because of my integrity you uphold me
    and set me in your presence forever.

Praise be to the Lord, the God of Israel,
    from everlasting to everlasting.
Amen and Amen.

JEREMIAH 1:4–5

The word of the Lord came to me, saying,

"Before I formed you in the womb I knew you,
    before you were born I set you apart.
    I appointed you as a prophet to the nations."

JOHN 17:24

Father, I want those you have given me to be with me where I am, and to see my glory, the glory you have given me because you loved me before the creation of the world.

Lord, before anything else existed, you were. You knew everyone and everything that would be. Please teach me to remember this truth. I want to ponder your glory.

Our God of Future Eternity

PSALM 48:14

For this God is our God for ever and ever;
   he will be our guide even to the end.

ISAIAH 46:8–10

Remember this, keep it in mind,
   take it to heart, you rebels.
Remember the former things, those of long ago;
   I am God, and there is no other;
   I am God, and there is none like me.
I make known the end from the beginning,
   from ancient times, what is still to come.

1 PETER 1:18–21

For you know that it was not with perishable things such as silver
or gold that you were redeemed from the empty way of life handed
down to you from your ancestors, but with the precious blood of Christ,
a lamb without blemish or defect. He was chosen before the creation of
the world, but was revealed in these last times for your sake. Through
him you believe in God, who raised him from the dead and glorified
him, and so your faith and hope are in God.

~~~

Nothing in the future is beyond God's knowledge, guidance, or power.

Jesus, the Eternal God with Us

PSALM 16:9–11

Therefore my heart is glad and my tongue rejoices;
    my body also will rest secure,
because you will not abandon me to the realm of the dead,
    nor will you let your faithful one see decay.
You make known to me the path of life;
    you will fill me with joy in your presence,
    with eternal pleasures at your right hand.

ISAIAH 57:15

For this is what the high and exalted One says—
    he who lives forever, whose name is holy:
"I live in a high and holy place,
    but also with the one who is contrite and lowly in spirit,
to revive the spirit of the lowly
    and to revive the heart of the contrite."

HEBREWS 13:8

Jesus Christ is the same yesterday and today and forever.

When have you felt that God is too high above or too holy to see you? Ask Him to remind you that Jesus became human to be with His people, and He will be with you today and forever.

God's Unfathomable Mystery

PSALM 92:4–5

You make me glad by your deeds, Lord;
  I sing for joy at what your hands have done.
How great are your works, Lord,
  how profound your thoughts!

JOB 11:7–9

Can you fathom the mysteries of God?
  Can you probe the limits of the Almighty?
They are higher than the heavens above—what can you do?
  They are deeper than the depths below—what can you know?
Their measure is longer than the earth
  and wider than the sea.

1 CORINTHIANS 2:14–16

The person without the Spirit does not accept the things that come from the Spirit of God but considers them foolishness, and cannot understand them because they are discerned only through the Spirit. The person with the Spirit makes judgments about all things, but such a person is not subject to merely human judgments, for,

"Who has known the mind of the Lord
  so as to instruct him?"

But we have the mind of Christ.

~~~~

Lord, you are higher than heaven and deeper than outer space. I will never know the end of you. Your infinite mystery is humbling, but thank you that I get to spend eternity getting to know you better.

Our God Clothed in Mystery

PSALM 97:1–4

The LORD reigns, let the earth be glad;
    let the distant shores rejoice.
Clouds and thick darkness surround him;
    righteousness and justice are the foundation of his throne.
Fire goes before him
    and consumes his foes on every side.
His lightning lights up the world;
    the earth sees and trembles.

EXODUS 20:18–19, 21

When the people saw the thunder and lightning and heard the trumpet and saw the mountain in smoke, they trembled with fear. They stayed at a distance and said to Moses, "Speak to us yourself and we will listen. But do not have God speak to us or we will die." . . .

The people remained at a distance, while Moses approached the thick darkness where God was.

MATTHEW 17:2, 5–6

There [Jesus] was transfigured before them. His face shone like the sun, and his clothes became as white as the light. . . .

While he was still speaking, a bright cloud covered them, and a voice from the cloud said, "This is my Son, whom I love; with him I am well pleased. Listen to him!"

When the disciples heard this, they fell facedown to the ground, terrified.

God reveals himself to His people, but He cannot be known completely or contained.

Our Limited Understanding
of God's Mysteries

PSALM 131:1

My heart is not proud, LORD,
   my eyes are not haughty;
I do not concern myself with great matters
   or things too wonderful for me.

JOB 15:7–9

Are you the first man ever born?
   Were you brought forth before the hills?
Do you listen in on God's council?
   Do you have a monopoly on wisdom?
What do you know that we do not know?
   What insights do you have that we do not have?

ACTS 1:6–7

Then they gathered around him and asked him, "Lord, are you at this time going to restore the kingdom to Israel?"

He said to them: "It is not for you to know the times or dates the Father has set by his own authority."

~~~~~

Where have you been able to rest in the mysteries of God's wisdom and timing? Pray and thank God that His purposes do not depend on your understanding.

The God Who Reveals His Mysteries

PSALM 25:14–15

> The LORD confides in those who fear him;
> he makes his covenant known to them.
> My eyes are ever on the LORD.

DANIEL 2:46–47

Then King Nebuchadnezzar fell prostrate before Daniel and paid him honor and ordered that an offering and incense be presented to him. The king said to Daniel, "Surely your God is the God of gods and the Lord of kings and a revealer of mysteries, for you were able to reveal this mystery."

COLOSSIANS 1:25–27

I have become its servant by the commission God gave me to present to you the word of God in its fullness—the mystery that has been kept hidden for ages and generations, but is now disclosed to the Lord's people. To them God has chosen to make known among the Gentiles the glorious riches of this mystery, which is Christ in you, the hope of glory.

~~~

Lord, thank you that you are revealing the fullness of your mystery, which is Christ inside your people. It's an incredible privilege that you dwell in me.

God's Mysterious Sovereignty

PSALM 148:7–10

Praise the LORD from the earth,
> you great sea creatures and all ocean depths,
lightning and hail, snow and clouds,
> stormy winds that do his bidding,
you mountains and all hills,
> fruit trees and all cedars,
wild animals and all cattle,
> small creatures and flying birds.

JOB 36:22–26

God is exalted in his power. . . .
Who has prescribed his ways for him,
> or said to him, "You have done wrong"?
Remember to extol his work,
> which people have praised in song.
All humanity has seen it;
> mortals gaze on it from afar.
How great is God—beyond our understanding!

EPHESIANS 3:7–9

I became a servant of this gospel by the gift of God's grace given me through the working of his power. Although I am less than the least of all the Lord's people, this grace was given me: to preach to the Gentiles the boundless riches of Christ, and to make plain to everyone the administration of this mystery, which for ages past was kept hidden in God, who created all things.

~~~

Even when you don't understand God's workings, He created all things and guides all things.

Searching Out God in the Secret Places

PSALM 63:6–7

On my bed I remember you;
    I think of you through the watches of the night.
Because you are my help,
    I sing in the shadow of your wings.

ISAIAH 45:2–3

I will go before you
    and will level the mountains;
I will break down gates of bronze
    and cut through bars of iron.
I will give you hidden treasures,
    riches stored in secret places,
so that you may know that I am the LORD,
    the God of Israel, who summons you by name.

1 PETER 1:10–12

Concerning this salvation, the prophets, who spoke of the grace that was to come to you, searched intently and with the greatest care, trying to find out the time and circumstances to which the Spirit of Christ in them was pointing when he predicted the sufferings of the Messiah and the glories that would follow. It was revealed to them that they were not serving themselves but you, when they spoke of the things that have now been told you by those who have preached the gospel to you by the Holy Spirit sent from heaven. Even angels long to look into these things.

What is something about God you've given up too quickly on understanding? Talk with Him about it, asking Him to strengthen you as you search intently for Him.

The Mysterious Provision
of Jesus Christ

PSALM 104:27–28

> All creatures look to you
> to give them their food at the proper time.
> When you give it to them,
> they gather it up;
> when you open your hand,
> they are satisfied with good things.

JOB 5:8–9

> But if I were you, I would appeal to God;
> I would lay my cause before him.
> He performs wonders that cannot be fathomed,
> miracles that cannot be counted.

1 TIMOTHY 3:16

Beyond all question, the mystery from which true godliness springs is great:

> He appeared in the flesh,
> was vindicated by the Spirit,
> was seen by angels,
> was preached among the nations,
> was believed on in the world,
> was taken up in glory.

~~~

Lord, the wonders of Jesus's life, death, resurrection, and ascension cannot be fathomed. Thank you for providing your Son and satisfying my needs through Him.

The Transcendent God Dwelling with His Creation

PSALM 57:5

> Be exalted, O God, above the heavens;
>> let your glory be over all the earth.

ISAIAH 66:1–2

> This is what the LORD says:
>
> "Heaven is my throne,
>> and the earth is my footstool.
> Where is the house you will build for me?
>> Where will my resting place be?
> Has not my hand made all these things,
>> and so they came into being?"
> declares the LORD.

COLOSSIANS 1:13–15

> For he has rescued us from the dominion of darkness and brought us into the kingdom of the Son he loves, in whom we have redemption, the forgiveness of sins. The Son is the image of the invisible God, the firstborn over all creation.

~~~

God transcends His creation, yet He chooses to dwell among and inside His people.

God Transcends Life and Death

PSALM 88:9–12

> I call to you, LORD, every day;
> > I spread out my hands to you.
> Do you show your wonders to the dead?
> > Do their spirits rise up and praise you?
> Is your love declared in the grave,
> > your faithfulness in Destruction?
> Are your wonders known in the place of darkness,
> > or your righteous deeds in the land of oblivion?

HOSEA 13:14

> I will deliver this people from the power of the grave;
> > I will redeem them from death.
> Where, O death, are your plagues?
> > Where, O grave, is your destruction?

1 CORINTHIANS 15:54–56

When the perishable has been clothed with the imperishable, and the mortal with immortality, then the saying that is written will come true: "Death has been swallowed up in victory."

> "Where, O death, is your victory?
> > Where, O death, is your sting?"

The sting of death is sin, and the power of sin is the law. But thanks be to God! He gives us the victory through our Lord Jesus Christ.

Have you lost someone, or are you anxious about losing someone, who you will see again in Christ? Thank God that He holds the victory over death.

God's Transcendent Power

PSALM 136:3–7

Give thanks to the Lord of lords:
  His love endures forever.

to him who alone does great wonders,
  His love endures forever.
who by his understanding made the heavens,
  His love endures forever.
who spread out the earth upon the waters,
  His love endures forever.
who made the great lights—
  His love endures forever.

JOB 26:12–14

By his power he churned up the sea;
  by his wisdom he cut Rahab to pieces.
By his breath the skies became fair;
  his hand pierced the gliding serpent.
And these are but the outer fringe of his works;
  how faint the whisper we hear of him!
  Who then can understand the thunder of his power?

COLOSSIANS 2:9–10

For in Christ all the fullness of the Deity lives in bodily form, and
in Christ you have been brought to fullness. He is the head over every
power and authority.

~~~~~

*Lord, your great wonders and thunderous power are so far beyond
what I can perceive or understand. I'm so glad that all your works
point to your enduring, unshakable love.*

Trinity

Praise God, from whom all blessings flow;

praise Him, all creatures here below;

praise Him above, ye heav'nly host;

praise Father, Son, and Holy Ghost. Amen.

Thomas Ken, 1674

The Trinity Creates

PSALM 33:6–9

By the word of the LORD the heavens were made,
   their starry host by the breath of his mouth.
He gathers the waters of the sea into jars;
   he puts the deep into storehouses.
Let all the earth fear the LORD;
   let all the people of the world revere him.
For he spoke, and it came to be;
   he commanded, and it stood firm.

GENESIS 1:1–2

In the beginning God created the heavens and the earth. Now the earth was formless and empty, darkness was over the surface of the deep, and the Spirit of God was hovering over the waters.

JOHN 5:19–21

Very truly I tell you, the Son can do nothing by himself; he can do only what he sees his Father doing, because whatever the Father does the Son also does. For the Father loves the Son and shows him all he does. Yes, and he will show him even greater works than these, so that you will be amazed. For just as the Father raises the dead and gives them life, even so the Son gives life to whom he is pleased to give it.

〜〜〜

The triune God—Father, Son, and Holy Spirit—made all of creation together.

JUNE 2

The Trinity Directs

PSALM 99:6–7

They called on the LORD
    and he answered them.
He spoke to them from the pillar of cloud;
    they kept his statutes and the decrees he gave them.

ISAIAH 48:16–17

"Come near me and listen to this:

"From the first announcement I have not spoken in secret;
    at the time it happens, I am there."

And now the Sovereign LORD has sent me,
    endowed with his Spirit.

This is what the LORD says—
    your Redeemer, the Holy One of Israel:
"I am the LORD your God,
    who teaches you what is best for you,
    who directs you in the way you should go."

MATTHEW 28:18–20

Then Jesus came to them and said, "All authority in heaven and on earth has been given to me. Therefore go and make disciples of all nations, baptizing them in the name of the Father and of the Son and of the Holy Spirit, and teaching them to obey everything I have commanded you. And surely I am with you always, to the very end of the age."

~~~~

When was a time you failed to listen to God's direction? Confess to Him, and thank Him for the presence and teaching of His Spirit in your life.

The Trinity Comes Near

PSALM 8:5–8

> You have made them a little lower than the angels
> and crowned them with glory and honor.
> You made them rulers over the works of your hands;
> you put everything under their feet:
> all flocks and herds,
> and the animals of the wild,
> the birds in the sky,
> and the fish in the sea,
> all that swim the paths of the seas.

GENESIS 18:1–3

The LORD appeared to Abraham near the great trees of Mamre while he was sitting at the entrance to his tent in the heat of the day. Abraham looked up and saw three men standing nearby. When he saw them, he hurried from the entrance of his tent to meet them and bowed low to the ground.

He said, "If I have found favor in your eyes, my lord, do not pass your servant by."

HEBREWS 2:8–9

At present we do not see everything subject to them. But we do see Jesus, who was made lower than the angels for a little while, now crowned with glory and honor because he suffered death, so that by the grace of God he might taste death for everyone.

~~~~

Lord, you are a holy, triune mystery I can't fully comprehend. Thank you for becoming like me and drawing near to me. I want to be freshly amazed by your glory and grace.

The Trinity Reveals His Glory

PSALM 97:5–6

The mountains melt like wax before the LORD,
    before the Lord of all the earth.
The heavens proclaim his righteousness,
    and all peoples see his glory.

EXODUS 23:20–21

See, I am sending an angel ahead of you to guard you along the way
and to bring you to the place I have prepared. Pay attention to him and
listen to what he says. Do not rebel against him; he will not forgive your
rebellion, since my Name is in him.

2 CORINTHIANS 3:14–18

To this day the same veil remains when the old covenant is read.
It has not been removed, because only in Christ is it taken away. Even
to this day when Moses is read, a veil covers their hearts. But whenever
anyone turns to the Lord, the veil is taken away. Now the Lord is the
Spirit, and where the Spirit of the Lord is, there is freedom. And we
all, who with unveiled faces contemplate the Lord's glory, are being
transformed into his image with ever-increasing glory, which comes
from the Lord, who is the Spirit.

~~~~~~

*Through the Father's command, the Son's work, and the Spirit's
freedom, the Trinity reveals His glory.*

The Trinity Delights

PSALM 149:2–4

> Let Israel rejoice in their Maker;
>   let the people of Zion be glad in their King.
> Let them praise his name with dancing
>   and make music to him with timbrel and harp.
> For the LORD takes delight in his people.

GENESIS 1:26–27

Then God said, "Let us make mankind in our image, in our likeness, so that they may rule over the fish in the sea and the birds in the sky, over the livestock and all the wild animals, and over all the creatures that move along the ground."

> So God created mankind in his own image,
>   in the image of God he created them;
>   male and female he created them.

MATTHEW 3:16–17

As soon as Jesus was baptized, he went up out of the water. At that moment heaven was opened, and he saw the Spirit of God descending like a dove and alighting on him. And a voice from heaven said, "This is my Son, whom I love; with him I am well pleased."

Where have you felt God's delight in you, or in the work and community found in His creation? Ask Him to make you more aware of His delight.

The Trinity Blesses

PSALM 29:10–11

The LORD sits enthroned over the flood;
    the LORD is enthroned as King forever.
The LORD gives strength to his people;
    the LORD blesses his people with peace.

NUMBERS 6:22–26

The LORD said to Moses, "Tell Aaron and his sons, 'This is how you are to bless the Israelites. Say to them:

""The LORD bless you
    and keep you;
the LORD make his face shine on you
    and be gracious to you;
the LORD turn his face toward you
    and give you peace.""

2 CORINTHIANS 13:14

May the grace of the Lord Jesus Christ, and the love of God, and the fellowship of the Holy Spirit be with you all.

～～

Lord, you are King forever. Please bless your people with grace, love, and peaceful fellowship. In the name of the Father, Son, and Holy Spirit.

The Trinity Overshadows

PSALM 99:1–3

> The LORD reigns,
>   let the nations tremble;
> he sits enthroned between the cherubim,
>   let the earth shake.
> Great is the LORD in Zion;
>   he is exalted over all the nations.
> Let them praise your great and awesome name—
>   he is holy.

1 CHRONICLES 28:18–19

[God] also gave him the plan for the chariot, that is, the cherubim of gold that spread their wings and overshadow the ark of the covenant of the LORD.

"All this," David said, "I have in writing as a result of the LORD's hand on me, and he enabled me to understand all the details of the plan."

LUKE 1:34–35

"How will this be," Mary asked the angel, "since I am a virgin?"

The angel answered, "The Holy Spirit will come on you, and the power of the Most High will overshadow you. So the holy one to be born will be called the Son of God."

~~~~

The power and purposes of the Trinity—Father, Son, and Spirit— are over all His creation.

God the Father

PSALM 89:25–27

> I will set his hand over the sea,
>> his right hand over the rivers.
> He will call out to me, "You are my Father,
>> my God, the Rock my Savior."
> And I will appoint him to be my firstborn,
>> the most exalted of the kings of the earth.

MALACHI 2:10

Do we not all have one Father? Did not one God create us? Why do we profane the covenant of our ancestors by being unfaithful to one another?

EPHESIANS 3:14–17

For this reason I kneel before the Father, from whom every family in heaven and on earth derives its name. I pray that out of his glorious riches he may strengthen you with power through his Spirit in your inner being, so that Christ may dwell in your hearts through faith.

How have your earthly father figures disappointed or hurt you? Talk with God about it, and ask Him to show you how He is your perfect Father.

Our Adopting Father

PSALM 68:4–5

Sing to God, sing in praise of his name,
 extol him who rides on the clouds;
 rejoice before him—his name is the LORD.
A father to the fatherless, a defender of widows,
 is God in his holy dwelling.

JEREMIAH 3:19

I myself said,

"How gladly would I treat you like my children
 and give you a pleasant land,
 the most beautiful inheritance of any nation.
I thought you would call me 'Father'
 and not turn away from following me."

ROMANS 8:14–17

For those who are led by the Spirit of God are the children of God.
The Spirit you received does not make you slaves, so that you live in fear
again; rather, the Spirit you received brought about your adoption to
sonship. And by him we cry, "*Abba*, Father." The Spirit himself testifies
with our spirit that we are God's children. Now if we are children, then
we are heirs—heirs of God and co-heirs with Christ, if indeed we share
in his sufferings in order that we may also share in his glory.

*Lord, thank you for adopting me as your own. I'm so grateful that
you want share yourself with me, teach me how to live in your family,
and give me an eternal inheritance.*

Our Caring Father

PSALM 95:6–7

Come, let us bow down in worship,
    let us kneel before the LORD our Maker;
for he is our God
      and we are the people of his pasture,
      the flock under his care.

DEUTERONOMY 1:29–31

Then I said to you, "Do not be terrified; do not be afraid of them. The LORD your God, who is going before you, will fight for you, as he did for you in Egypt, before your very eyes, and in the wilderness. There you saw how the LORD your God carried you, as a father carries his son, all the way you went until you reached this place."

LUKE 11:11–13

Which of you fathers, if your son asks for a fish, will give him a snake instead? Or if he asks for an egg, will give him a scorpion? If you then, though you are evil, know how to give good gifts to your children, how much more will your Father in heaven give the Holy Spirit to those who ask him!

~~~~~~~

You don't need to be afraid because God your Father cares for you and gives you His good Spirit.

Our Disciplining Father

PSALM 27:10–11

Though my father and mother forsake me,
    the LORD will receive me.
Teach me your way, LORD;
    lead me in a straight path.

PROVERBS 3:11–12

My son, do not despise the LORD's discipline,
    and do not resent his rebuke,
because the LORD disciplines those he loves,
    as a father the son he delights in.

HEBREWS 12:7–9

Endure hardship as discipline; God is treating you as his children. For what children are not disciplined by their father? If you are not disciplined—and everyone undergoes discipline—then you are not legitimate, not true sons and daughters at all. Moreover, we have all had human fathers who disciplined us and we respected them for it. How much more should we submit to the Father of spirits and live!

What word or phrase from the passages above stood out to you? Pause to talk with God about it.

Our Forgiving Father

PSALM 103:13–14

As a father has compassion on his children,
 so the LORD has compassion on those who fear him;
for he knows how we are formed,
 he remembers that we are dust.

ZEPHANIAH 3:14–15

Sing, Daughter Zion;
 shout aloud, Israel!
Be glad and rejoice with all your heart,
 Daughter Jerusalem!
The LORD has taken away your punishment,
 he has turned back your enemy.
The LORD, the King of Israel, is with you;
 never again will you fear any harm.

1 JOHN 3:1, 5

See what great love the Father has lavished on us, that we should be called children of God! And that is what we are! The reason the world does not know us is that it did not know him. . . .

But you know that he appeared so that he might take away our sins. And in him is no sin.

~~~~~

Lord, you are full of compassion, a Father who forgives His children and longs for reconnection. Remind me when I've sinned and feel ashamed that you will always be my Father.

Our Nurturing Father

PSALM 127:3–5

Children are a heritage from the LORD,
  offspring a reward from him.
Like arrows in the hands of a warrior
  are children born in one's youth.
Blessed is the man
  whose quiver is full of them.
They will not be put to shame
  when they contend with their opponents in court.

HOSEA 11:1, 3

When Israel was a child, I loved him,
  and out of Egypt I called my son. . . .
It was I who taught Ephraim to walk,
  taking them by the arms;
but they did not realize
  it was I who healed them.

GALATIANS 4:6–7

Because you are his sons, God sent the Spirit of his Son into our hearts, the Spirit who calls out, "*Abba*, Father." So you are no longer a slave, but God's child; and since you are his child, God has made you also an heir.

~~~~~

God your Father takes you by the arms, teaching you to walk in His ways and making you His heir.

The Father Keeps His Own

PSALM 146:8–9

> The LORD lifts up those who are bowed down,
>> the LORD loves the righteous.
> The LORD watches over the foreigner
>> and sustains the fatherless and the widow,
>> but he frustrates the ways of the wicked.

ISAIAH 64:8–9

> Yet you, LORD, are our Father.
>> We are the clay, you are the potter;
>> we are all the work of your hand.
> Do not be angry beyond measure, LORD;
>> do not remember our sins forever.
> Oh, look on us, we pray,
>> for we are all your people.

1 THESSALONIANS 3:13

May [the Lord] strengthen your hearts so that you will be blameless and holy in the presence of our God and Father when our Lord Jesus comes with all his holy ones.

~~~~~

Have you ever felt that God was holding on to His anger or your sin? Thank Him that He is making you blameless and holy, and that you are what He's holding on to.

God the Son

PSALM 2:7–8

I will proclaim the LORD's decree:

He said to me, "You are my son;
> today I have become your father.
Ask me,
> and I will make the nations your inheritance,
> the ends of the earth your possession."

ISAIAH 9:6–7

For to us a child is born,
> to us a son is given,
> and the government will be on his shoulders.
And he will be called
> Wonderful Counselor, Mighty God,
> Everlasting Father, Prince of Peace.
Of the greatness of his government and peace
> there will be no end.

JOHN 1:14

The Word became flesh and made his dwelling among us. We have seen his glory, the glory of the one and only Son, who came from the Father, full of grace and truth.

~~~~~

Lord Jesus, thank you that you came from the Father to dwell among your creation. I pray eagerly for your kingdom, for your government of peace that will encompass the whole world.

The Self-Giving Son

PSALM 22:1–2

My God, my God, why have you forsaken me?
Why are you so far from saving me,
so far from my cries of anguish?
My God, I cry out by day, but you do not answer,
by night, but I find no rest.

ISAIAH 53:4–6

Surely he took up our pain
and bore our suffering,
yet we considered him punished by God,
stricken by him, and afflicted.
But he was pierced for our transgressions,
he was crushed for our iniquities;
the punishment that brought us peace was on him,
and by his wounds we are healed.
We all, like sheep, have gone astray,
each of us has turned to our own way;
and the Lord has laid on him
the iniquity of us all.

1 JOHN 2:1–2

But if anybody does sin, we have an advocate with the Father—Jesus
Christ, the Righteous One. He is the atoning sacrifice for our sins, and
not only for ours but also for the sins of the whole world.

~~~~~

*Jesus took the sins and suffering of the world to the cross so you could
be healed and reconciled in peace to God.*

The Son of the Most High

PSALM 82:5–7

> The "gods" know nothing, they understand nothing.
>> They walk about in darkness;
>> all the foundations of the earth are shaken.
> I said, "You are 'gods';
>> you are all sons of the Most High."
> But you will die like mere mortals;
>> you will fall like every other ruler.

DANIEL 7:13–14

In my vision at night I looked, and there before me was one like a son of man, coming with the clouds of heaven. He approached the Ancient of Days and was led into his presence. He was given authority, glory and sovereign power; all nations and peoples of every language worshiped him. His dominion is an everlasting dominion that will not pass away, and his kingdom is one that will never be destroyed.

JOHN 10:34–36

Jesus answered them, "Is it not written in your Law, 'I have said you are "gods"'? If he called them 'gods,' to whom the word of God came— and Scripture cannot be set aside—what about the one whom the Father set apart as his very own and sent into the world? Why then do you accuse me of blasphemy because I said, 'I am God's Son'?"

~~~

What do you feel knowing that Jesus shares all authority, glory, and sovereignty with His Father and the Spirit? Pray to Jesus and tell Him about it.

The Mission of the Son

PSALM 80:17, 19

> Let your hand rest on the man at your right hand,
>> the son of man you have raised up for yourself. . . .

> Restore us, Lord God Almighty;
>> make your face shine on us,
>> that we may be saved.

ISAIAH 61:1–2

> The Spirit of the Sovereign Lord is on me,
>> because the Lord has anointed me
>> to proclaim good news to the poor.
> He has sent me to bind up the brokenhearted,
>> to proclaim freedom for the captives
>> and release from darkness for the prisoners,
> to proclaim the year of the Lord's favor.

LUKE 4:17–18, 20–21

The scroll of the prophet Isaiah was handed to [Jesus]. Unrolling it, he found the place where it is written:

> "The Spirit of the Lord is on me,
>> because he has anointed me
>> to proclaim good news to the poor. . . ."

The eyes of everyone in the synagogue were fastened on him. He began by saying to them, "Today this scripture is fulfilled in your hearing."

～～～

Lord Jesus, your kingdom brings restoration for the poor, broken-hearted, imprisoned, and enslaved. Thank you for coming to break the power of sin.

The Sacrificed Son

PSALM 31:3-5

Since you are my rock and my fortress,
    for the sake of your name lead and guide me.
Keep me free from the trap that is set for me,
    for you are my refuge.
Into your hands I commit my spirit;
    deliver me, Lord, my faithful God.

ZECHARIAH 12:10

And I will pour out on the house of David and the inhabitants of Jerusalem a spirit of grace and supplication. They will look on me, the one they have pierced, and they will mourn for him as one mourns for an only child, and grieve bitterly for him as one grieves for a firstborn son.

GALATIANS 2:19-20

For through the law I died to the law so that I might live for God. I have been crucified with Christ and I no longer live, but Christ lives in me. The life I now live in the body, I live by faith in the Son of God, who loved me and gave himself for me.

~~~~~

Through Jesus's crucifixion and resurrection, you died with Him and He now lives in you.

The Eternal Reign of the Son

PSALM 110:1

The LORD says to my lord:

"Sit at my right hand
    until I make your enemies
    a footstool for your feet."

JEREMIAH 23:5–6

"The days are coming," declares the LORD,
    "when I will raise up for David a righteous Branch,
a King who will reign wisely
    and do what is just and right in the land.
In his days Judah will be saved
    and Israel will live in safety.
This is the name by which he will be called:
    The LORD Our Righteous Savior."

1 CORINTHIANS 15:27–28

For he "has put everything under his feet." Now when it says that "everything" has been put under him, it is clear that this does not include God himself, who put everything under Christ. When he has done this, then the Son himself will be made subject to him who put everything under him, so that God may be all in all.

~

In what area of your life are you living as if Jesus weren't King? Confess this to God, and ask Him to teach you how to participate more fully in His wise, just, and righteous kingdom.

The Love of the Son, Sent by the Father

PSALM 45:7

You love righteousness and hate wickedness;
therefore God, your God, has set you above your companions
by anointing you with the oil of joy.

2 SAMUEL 7:12–14

When your days are over and you rest with your ancestors, I will
raise up your offspring to succeed you, your own flesh and blood, and I
will establish his kingdom. He is the one who will build a house for my
Name, and I will establish the throne of his kingdom forever. I will be
his father, and he will be my son.

JOHN 3:16–17

For God so loved the world that he gave his one and only Son, that
whoever believes in him shall not perish but have eternal life. For God
did not send his Son into the world to condemn the world, but to save
the world through him.

~~~~~~

*Lord, thank you for loving me and sending your Son to save the
world so I can live forever in relationship with you. You promised
your Son so long ago; I'm grateful for your faithfulness.*

God the Holy Spirit

PSALM 104:30–32

> When you send your Spirit,
> > they are created,
> > and you renew the face of the ground.
>
> May the glory of the LORD endure forever;
> > may the LORD rejoice in his works—
> he who looks at the earth, and it trembles,
> > who touches the mountains, and they smoke.

JOB 33:3–4

> My words come from an upright heart;
> > my lips sincerely speak what I know.
> The Spirit of God has made me;
> > the breath of the Almighty gives me life.

JOHN 4:23–24

Yet a time is coming and has now come when the true worshipers will worship the Father in the Spirit and in truth, for they are the kind of worshipers the Father seeks. God is spirit, and his worshipers must worship in the Spirit and in truth.

~~~~~

God is Spirit, and the Spirit of God gives life.

The Holy Spirit Inspires

PSALM 143:8–10

Show me the way I should go,
    for to you I entrust my life.
Rescue me from my enemies, LORD,
    for I hide myself in you.
Teach me to do your will,
    for you are my God;
may your good Spirit
    lead me on level ground.

EXODUS 31:1–5

Then the LORD said to Moses, "See, I have chosen Bezalel son of Uri, the son of Hur, of the tribe of Judah, and I have filled him with the Spirit of God, with wisdom, with understanding, with knowledge and with all kinds of skills—to make artistic designs for work in gold, silver and bronze, to cut and set stones, to work in wood, and to engage in all kinds of crafts."

ACTS 2:1–4

When the day of Pentecost came, they were all together in one place. Suddenly a sound like the blowing of a violent wind came from heaven and filled the whole house where they were sitting. They saw what seemed to be tongues of fire that separated and came to rest on each of them. All of them were filled with the Holy Spirit and began to speak in other tongues as the Spirit enabled them.

Where have you seen the Spirit's inspiration in your life or in the life of another believer? Thank Him for His teaching, creativity, and empowerment.

The Holy Spirit Convicts

PSALM 18:15

The valleys of the sea were exposed
    and the foundations of the earth laid bare
at your rebuke, Lord,
    at the blast of breath from your nostrils.

MICAH 3:7–8

"The seers will be ashamed
    and the diviners disgraced.
They will all cover their faces
    because there is no answer from God."
But as for me, I am filled with power,
    with the Spirit of the Lord,
    and with justice and might,
to declare to Jacob his transgression,
    to Israel his sin.

JOHN 16:7–11

Unless I go away, the Advocate will not come to you; but if I go, I will send him to you. When he comes, he will prove the world to be in the wrong about sin and righteousness and judgment: about sin, because people do not believe in me; about righteousness, because I am going to the Father, where you can see me no longer; and about judgment, because the prince of this world now stands condemned.

Lord, I know I sin against you and against others even though I am yours. Forgive me. Thank you that your Spirit is inside me to convict me and turn me back to you.

The Holy Spirit Judges

PSALM 106:32–33

By the waters of Meribah they angered the LORD,
    and trouble came to Moses because of them;
for they rebelled against the Spirit of God,
    and rash words came from Moses' lips.

ISAIAH 11:3–5

He will not judge by what he sees with his eyes,
    or decide by what he hears with his ears;
but with righteousness he will judge the needy,
    with justice he will give decisions for the poor of the earth.
He will strike the earth with the rod of his mouth;
    with the breath of his lips he will slay the wicked.
Righteousness will be his belt
    and faithfulness the sash around his waist.

GALATIANS 5:19–23

The acts of the flesh are obvious: sexual immorality, impurity and debauchery; idolatry and witchcraft; hatred, discord, jealousy, fits of rage, selfish ambition, dissensions, factions and envy; drunkenness, orgies, and the like. I warn you, as I did before, that those who live like this will not inherit the kingdom of God.

But the fruit of the Spirit is love, joy, peace, forbearance, kindness, goodness, faithfulness, gentleness and self-control. Against such things there is no law.

The Holy Spirit judges righteously and faithfully to condemn the acts of the flesh, in order to produce the fruit of love and joy in your life.

The Holy Spirit Cleanses

PSALM 51:10–12

Create in me a pure heart, O God,
    and renew a steadfast spirit within me.
Do not cast me from your presence
    or take your Holy Spirit from me.
Restore to me the joy of your salvation
    and grant me a willing spirit, to sustain me.

EZEKIEL 36:26–28

I will give you a new heart and put a new spirit in you; I will remove from you your heart of stone and give you a heart of flesh. And I will put my Spirit in you and move you to follow my decrees and be careful to keep my laws. Then you will live in the land I gave your ancestors; you will be my people, and I will be your God.

1 CORINTHIANS 6:11

But you were washed, you were sanctified, you were justified in the name of the Lord Jesus Christ and by the Spirit of our God.

What do you need cleansing from? Talk with the Holy Spirit about it, asking Him to renew your spirit and to remind you that He has already justified you.

The Holy Spirit Indwells

PSALM 135:15–18

> The idols of the nations are silver and gold,
> made by human hands.
> They have mouths, but cannot speak,
> eyes, but cannot see.
> They have ears, but cannot hear,
> nor is there breath in their mouths.
> Those who make them will be like them,
> and so will all who trust in them.

EZEKIEL 37:7–9

As I was prophesying, there was a noise, a rattling sound, and the bones came together, bone to bone. I looked, and tendons and flesh appeared on them and skin covered them, but there was no breath in them.

Then he said to me, "Prophesy to the breath; prophesy, son of man, and say to it, 'This is what the Sovereign LORD says: Come, breath, from the four winds and breathe into these slain, that they may live.'"

JOHN 14:15–17

If you love me, keep my commands. And I will ask the Father, and he will give you another advocate to help you and be with you forever— the Spirit of truth. The world cannot accept him, because it neither sees him nor knows him. But you know him, for he lives with you and will be in you.

~~~

Lord, I'm humbled that your Spirit dwells in me, giving me life and showing me how to love you and love others. It's a privilege to belong to the one true God.

The Holy Spirit Brings Together

PSALM 67:3–5

> May the peoples praise you, God;
>   may all the peoples praise you.
> May the nations be glad and sing for joy,
>   for you rule the peoples with equity
>   and guide the nations of the earth.
> May the peoples praise you, God;
>   may all the peoples praise you.

HAGGAI 2:4–5

"Be strong, all you people of the land," declares the LORD, "and work. For I am with you," declares the LORD Almighty. "This is what I covenanted with you when you came out of Egypt. And my Spirit remains among you. Do not fear."

1 CORINTHIANS 12:12–14

Just as a body, though one, has many parts, but all its many parts form one body, so it is with Christ. For we were all baptized by one Spirit so as to form one body—whether Jews or Gentiles, slave or free—and we were all given the one Spirit to drink. Even so the body is not made up of one part but of many.

～～～

The Holy Spirit brings unity to the diverse body of Christ, which He is drawing from every nation and people of the earth.

The Triune God Intercedes
for His People

PSALM 110:4

The LORD has sworn
and will not change his mind:
"You are a priest forever,
in the order of Melchizedek."

JEREMIAH 31:9

They will come with weeping;
they will pray as I bring them back.
I will lead them beside streams of water
on a level path where they will not stumble,
because I am Israel's father,
and Ephraim is my firstborn son.

ROMANS 8:26–27

In the same way, the Spirit helps us in our weakness. We do not
know what we ought to pray for, but the Spirit himself intercedes for
us through wordless groans. And he who searches our hearts knows
the mind of the Spirit, because the Spirit intercedes for God's people
in accordance with the will of God.

~

When have you felt the Spirit interceding for you in the past?
Thank Him that through Jesus's sacrifice, the Father's leading,
and the Spirit's advocacy, God is working out His will in your life.

The Trinity's Everlasting Kingdom

PSALM 10:16–18

The LORD is King for ever and ever;
    the nations will perish from his land.
You, LORD, hear the desire of the afflicted;
    you encourage them, and you listen to their cry,
defending the fatherless and the oppressed.

2 SAMUEL 23:2–4

The Spirit of the LORD spoke through me;
    his word was on my tongue. . . .
"When one rules over people in righteousness,
    when he rules in the fear of God,
he is like the light of morning at sunrise
    on a cloudless morning,
like the brightness after rain
    that brings grass from the earth."

HEBREWS 1:8–9

But about the Son he says,

"Your throne, O God, will last for ever and ever;
    a scepter of justice will be the scepter of your kingdom.
You have loved righteousness and hated wickedness;
    therefore God, your God, has set you above your companions
    by anointing you with the oil of joy."

Lord, I'm so grateful you're establishing an eternal kingdom of righteousness over your creation. Any human kingdom that reigned forever would be disastrous, but you are the perfect triune King.

Creative

For the beauty of the earth,

for the glory of the skies,

for the love which from our birth

over and around us lies.

For the beauty of each hour
of the day and of the night,
hill and vale and tree and flower,
sun and moon and stars of light.

For the joy of human love,
brother, sister, parent, child,
friends on earth, and friends above,
for all gentle thoughts and mild.

For each perfect gift of thine
to our race so freely given,
graces, human and divine,
flowers of earth and buds of heaven.

Lord of all, to thee we raise
this, our hymn of grateful praise.

Folliott Sandford Pierpoint, 1864

Our Creator God

PSALM 19:1–4

> The heavens declare the glory of God;
>> the skies proclaim the work of his hands.
> Day after day they pour forth speech;
>> night after night they reveal knowledge.
> They have no speech, they use no words;
>> no sound is heard from them.
> Yet their voice goes out into all the earth,
>> their words to the ends of the world.

ISAIAH 45:18

> For this is what the LORD says—
> he who created the heavens,
>> he is God;
> he who fashioned and made the earth,
>> he founded it;
> he did not create it to be empty,
>> but formed it to be inhabited—
> he says:
> "I am the LORD,
>> and there is no other."

HEBREWS 3:3–4

Jesus has been found worthy of greater honor than Moses, just as the builder of a house has greater honor than the house itself. For every house is built by someone, but God is the builder of everything.

God created everything that is, showcasing His creativity, glory, and wisdom.

The Handiwork of Our Creator

PSALM 119:73

Your hands made me and formed me;
give me understanding to learn your commands.

GENESIS 2:20–23

But for Adam no suitable helper was found. So the LORD God caused the man to fall into a deep sleep; and while he was sleeping, he took one of the man's ribs and then closed up the place with flesh. Then the LORD God made a woman from the rib he had taken out of the man, and he brought her to the man.

The man said,

"This is now bone of my bones
and flesh of my flesh;
she shall be called 'woman,'
for she was taken out of man."

EPHESIANS 2:8–10

For it is by grace you have been saved, through faith—and this is not from yourselves, it is the gift of God—not by works, so that no one can boast. For we are God's handiwork, created in Christ Jesus to do good works, which God prepared in advance for us to do.

~~~~~

Where are you failing to see the image of God in the people around you? Confess this to God, and ask Him to show you how He sees His handiwork.

Interdependence within God's Creativity

PSALM 143:5-6

I remember the days of long ago;
    I meditate on all your works
    and consider what your hands have done.
I spread out my hands to you;
    I thirst for you like a parched land.

GENESIS 5:1-2

When God created mankind, he made them in the likeness of God. He created them male and female and blessed them. And he named them "Mankind" when they were created.

1 CORINTHIANS 11:11-12

Nevertheless, in the Lord woman is not independent of man, nor is man independent of woman. For as woman came from man, so also man is born of woman. But everything comes from God.

~~~

Lord, thank you for not making me to be alone. Please teach me to cultivate healthy, interdependent relationships, where I love others as I love myself.

God's Creative Provision

PSALM 124:6–8

Praise be to the LORD,
    who has not let us be torn by their teeth.
We have escaped like a bird
    from the fowler's snare;
the snare has been broken,
    and we have escaped.
Our help is in the name of the LORD,
    the Maker of heaven and earth.

ISAIAH 54:4–5

You will forget the shame of your youth
    and remember no more the reproach of your widowhood.
For your Maker is your husband—
    the LORD Almighty is his name—
the Holy One of Israel is your Redeemer;
    he is called the God of all the earth.

LUKE 12:27–28

Consider how the wild flowers grow. They do not labor or spin. Yet I tell you, not even Solomon in all his splendor was dressed like one of these. If that is how God clothes the grass of the field, which is here today, and tomorrow is thrown into the fire, how much more will he clothe you!

God provides everyday necessities, rescue, and intimate relationship—in ways only He'd think of.

Creation's Proper Response
to Its Creator

PSALM 148:2–6

Praise him, all his angels;
    praise him, all his heavenly hosts.
Praise him, sun and moon;
    praise him, all you shining stars.
Praise him, you highest heavens
    and you waters above the skies.

Let them praise the name of the LORD,
    for at his command they were created,
and he established them for ever and ever—
    he issued a decree that will never pass away.

ECCLESIASTES 12:1–2

Remember your Creator
    in the days of your youth,
before the days of trouble come
        and the years approach when you will say,
    "I find no pleasure in them"—
before the sun and the light
        and the moon and the stars grow dark,
        and the clouds return after the rain.

1 TIMOTHY 4:4–5

For everything God created is good, and nothing is to be rejected if it is received with thanksgiving, because it is consecrated by the word of God and prayer.

What good thing has God created that you can praise Him for today? Pause to pray right now.

The Light of God's Creativity

PSALM 104:19–22

He made the moon to mark the seasons,
   and the sun knows when to go down.
You bring darkness, it becomes night,
   and all the beasts of the forest prowl.
The lions roar for their prey
   and seek their food from God.
The sun rises, and they steal away;
   they return and lie down in their dens.

GENESIS 1:3–5

And God said, "Let there be light," and there was light. God saw that the light was good, and he separated the light from the darkness. God called the light "day," and the darkness he called "night." And there was evening, and there was morning—the first day.

JOHN 1:6–10

There was a man sent from God whose name was John. He came as a witness to testify concerning that light, so that through him all might believe. He himself was not the light; he came only as a witness to the light.

The true light that gives light to everyone was coming into the world. He was in the world, and though the world was made through him, the world did not recognize him.

～～～

Lord, you created light with a word, and you are the Word that gives light to everyone. Jesus, please be the light by which I see everything as it truly is.

Our Re-Creating God

PSALM 134

> Praise the LORD, all you servants of the LORD
>> who minister by night in the house of the LORD.
> Lift up your hands in the sanctuary
>> and praise the LORD.
>
> May the LORD bless you from Zion,
>> he who is the Maker of heaven and earth.

ISAIAH 43:19–21

> See, I am doing a new thing!
>> Now it springs up; do you not perceive it?
> I am making a way in the wilderness
>> and streams in the wasteland.
> The wild animals honor me,
>> the jackals and the owls,
> because I provide water in the wilderness
>> and streams in the wasteland,
> to give drink to my people, my chosen,
>> the people I formed for myself
>> that they may proclaim my praise.

REVELATION 21:5–7

He who was seated on the throne said, "I am making everything new! . . . It is done. I am the Alpha and the Omega, the Beginning and the End. To the thirsty I will give water without cost from the spring of the water of life. Those who are victorious will inherit all this, and I will be their God and they will be my children."

~~~~~~

God is re-creating all the broken, lifeless places in His creation that have been damaged by sin.

The Creative, Creating Word of God

PSALM 119:130–132

The unfolding of your words gives light;
    it gives understanding to the simple.
I open my mouth and pant,
    longing for your commands.
Turn to me and have mercy on me,
    as you always do to those who love your name.

GENESIS 1:14–16, 18

And God said, "Let there be lights in the vault of the sky to separate the day from the night, and let them serve as signs to mark sacred times, and days and years, and let them be lights in the vault of the sky to give light on the earth." And it was so. God made two great lights—the greater light to govern the day and the lesser light to govern the night. . . . And God saw that it was good.

1 PETER 1:23–25

For you have been born again, not of perishable seed, but of imperishable, through the living and enduring word of God. For,

"All people are like grass,
    and all their glory is like the flowers of the field;
the grass withers and the flowers fall,
    but the word of the Lord endures forever."

~~~~~

When have you ignored God's words and the life they offer?
Talk with Him about it, thanking Him that His word endures
forever and has already given you a new birth into imperishable life.

God's Instructing, Illuminating Word

PSALM 119:105–106

> Your word is a lamp for my feet,
> a light on my path.
> I have taken an oath and confirmed it,
> that I will follow your righteous laws.

PROVERBS 4:20–22

> My son, pay attention to what I say;
> turn your ear to my words.
> Do not let them out of your sight,
> keep them within your heart;
> for they are life to those who find them
> and health to one's whole body.

MATTHEW 7:24–25

Therefore everyone who hears these words of mine and puts them into practice is like a wise man who built his house on the rock. The rain came down, the streams rose, and the winds blew and beat against that house; yet it did not fall, because it had its foundation on the rock.

Lord, thank you for your words, which guide me with light and righteousness. I want to build my life on your rock-solid wisdom.

The Life-Ordering Wisdom of God's Words

PSALM 119:9–12

How can a young person stay on the path of purity?
    By living according to your word.
I seek you with all my heart;
    do not let me stray from your commands.
I have hidden your word in my heart
    that I might not sin against you.
Praise be to you, LORD;
    teach me your decrees.

JOB 23:11–12

My feet have closely followed his steps;
    I have kept to his way without turning aside.
I have not departed from the commands of his lips;
    I have treasured the words of his mouth more than my
    daily bread.

2 TIMOTHY 3:14–17

But as for you, continue in what you have learned and have become convinced of, because you know those from whom you learned it, and how from infancy you have known the Holy Scriptures, which are able to make you wise for salvation through faith in Christ Jesus. All Scripture is God-breathed and is useful for teaching, rebuking, correcting and training in righteousness, so that the servant of God may be thoroughly equipped for every good work.

~~~~~~

God's commands teach you the best way to order all your actions, words, and relationships.

God's Eternal Word

PSALM 119:159–160

See how I love your precepts;
     preserve my life, LORD, in accordance with your love.
All your words are true;
     all your righteous laws are eternal.

EZEKIEL 12:28

This is what the Sovereign LORD says: None of my words will
be delayed any longer; whatever I say will be fulfilled, declares the
Sovereign LORD.

MATTHEW 24:32–35

Now learn this lesson from the fig tree: As soon as its twigs get
tender and its leaves come out, you know that summer is near. Even so,
when you see all these things, you know that it is near, right at the door.
Truly I tell you, this generation will certainly not pass away until all
these things have happened. Heaven and earth will pass away, but my
words will never pass away.

~~~~~

What word or phrase from the passages above stood out to you?
Pause to talk with God about it.

God's Perfect Word

PSALM 12:2, 6

Everyone lies to their neighbor;
    they flatter with their lips
    but harbor deception in their hearts. . . .

[But] the words of the LORD are flawless,
    like silver purified in a crucible,
    like gold refined seven times.

PROVERBS 30:5–6

Every word of God is flawless;
    he is a shield to those who take refuge in him.
Do not add to his words,
    or he will rebuke you and prove you a liar.

HEBREWS 4:12

For the word of God is alive and active. Sharper than any double-edged sword, it penetrates even to dividing soul and spirit, joints and marrow; it judges the thoughts and attitudes of the heart.

~~~~~

Lord, there is nothing untrue or harmful in your commands. Please use your Word to show me the untruths and harm in my heart, and replace them with your life and love.

God's Life-Sustaining Word

PSALM 130:5–6

I wait for the LORD, my whole being waits,
and in his word I put my hope.
I wait for the Lord
more than watchmen wait for the morning,
more than watchmen wait for the morning.

JEREMIAH 15:16

When your words came, I ate them;
they were my joy and my heart's delight,
for I bear your name,
LORD God Almighty.

MATTHEW 4:1–4

Then Jesus was led by the Spirit into the wilderness to be tempted by the devil. After fasting forty days and forty nights, he was hungry. The tempter came to him and said, "If you are the Son of God, tell these stones to become bread."

Jesus answered, "It is written: 'Man shall not live on bread alone, but on every word that comes from the mouth of God.'"

God's words created life in the beginning, and His words continue to sustain your life now and forever.

Jesus, the Incarnate Word of God

PSALM 107:19–21

Then they cried to the LORD in their trouble,
  and he saved them from their distress.
He sent out his word and healed them;
  he rescued them from the grave.
Let them give thanks to the LORD for his unfailing love
  and his wonderful deeds for mankind.

ISAIAH 55:10–11

As the rain and the snow
  come down from heaven,
and do not return to it
  without watering the earth
and making it bud and flourish,
  so that it yields seed for the sower and bread for the eater,
so is my word that goes out from my mouth:
  It will not return to me empty,
but will accomplish what I desire
  and achieve the purpose for which I sent it.

HEBREWS 1:1–3

In the past God spoke to our ancestors through the prophets at many times and in various ways, but in these last days he has spoken to us by his Son, whom he appointed heir of all things, and through whom also he made the universe. The Son is the radiance of God's glory and the exact representation of his being, sustaining all things by his powerful word.

In what ways are you living as if Jesus has not rescued you or won't accomplish His desires? Thank Him that He created the universe, sustains it, and is capable of doing what He says.

The God Who Makes Peace

PSALM 4:6–8

> Many, LORD, are asking, "Who will bring us prosperity?"
>> Let the light of your face shine on us.
> Fill my heart with joy
>> when their grain and new wine abound.
>
> In peace I will lie down and sleep,
>> for you alone, LORD,
>> make me dwell in safety.

ISAIAH 32:17–18

> The fruit of that righteousness will be peace;
>> its effect will be quietness and confidence forever.
> My people will live in peaceful dwelling places,
>> in secure homes,
>> in undisturbed places of rest.

ROMANS 5:1–2

> Therefore, since we have been justified through faith, we have peace with God through our Lord Jesus Christ, through whom we have gained access by faith into this grace in which we now stand.

~~~~~~

Lord, you have created so many good things, including peace between me and you and peace between me and the people around me. Thank you for making peace possible through your Son.

God Creates Peace from Chaos

PSALM 74:13–14, 16–17

> It was you who split open the sea by your power;
>> you broke the heads of the monster in the waters.
>
> It was you who crushed the heads of Leviathan
>> and gave it as food to the creatures of the desert. . . .
>
> The day is yours, and yours also the night;
>> you established the sun and moon.
>
> It was you who set all the boundaries of the earth.

ISAIAH 55:12–13

> You will go out in joy
>> and be led forth in peace;
>
> the mountains and hills
>> will burst into song before you,
>
> and all the trees of the field
>> will clap their hands.
>
> Instead of the thornbush will grow the juniper,
>> and instead of briers the myrtle will grow.
>
> This will be for the LORD's renown,
>> for an everlasting sign,
>> that will endure forever.

1 CORINTHIANS 14:31–33

> For you can all prophesy in turn so that everyone may be instructed and encouraged. The spirits of prophets are subject to the control of prophets. For God is not a God of disorder but of peace—as in all the congregations of the Lord's people.

~~~

As God formed creation out of the formless void, so He creates peace out of the world's disorder.

God Creates Peace through Teaching His Commands

PSALM 119:165–167

Great peace have those who love your law,
  and nothing can make them stumble.
I wait for your salvation, Lord,
  and I follow your commands.
I obey your statutes,
  for I love them greatly.

MALACHI 2:5–6

My covenant was with him, a covenant of life and peace, and I gave them to him; this called for reverence and he revered me and stood in awe of my name. True instruction was in his mouth and nothing false was found on his lips. He walked with me in peace and uprightness, and turned many from sin.

JOHN 14:25–27

All this I have spoken while still with you. But the Advocate, the Holy Spirit, whom the Father will send in my name, will teach you all things and will remind you of everything I have said to you. Peace I leave with you; my peace I give you. I do not give to you as the world gives. Do not let your hearts be troubled and do not be afraid.

～～～

Which commands of God can you practice today to cultivate peace in your relationships? Pray and ask the Holy Spirit to lead you in His peace.

God's Peace Creates New Patterns

PSALM 34:12–14

Whoever of you loves life
    and desires to see many good days,
keep your tongue from evil
    and your lips from telling lies.
Turn from evil and do good;
    seek peace and pursue it.

LEVITICUS 26:3–4, 6

If you follow my decrees and are careful to obey my commands, I will send you rain in its season, and the ground will yield its crops and the trees their fruit. . . .

I will grant peace in the land, and you will lie down and no one will make you afraid.

1 PETER 3:9–11

Do not repay evil with evil or insult with insult. On the contrary, repay evil with blessing, because to this you were called so that you may inherit a blessing. For,

"Whoever would love life
    and see good days
must keep their tongue from evil
    and their lips from deceitful speech.
They must turn from evil and do good;
    they must seek peace and pursue it."

~~~~~

Lord, thank you that you are undoing my prideful patterns of repaying evil with evil and insult with insult. Please teach me to follow your Word and to pursue peace in my life and relationships.

God's Peace Creates
New Relationships

PSALM 122:6–9

Pray for the peace of Jerusalem:
    "May those who love you be secure.
May there be peace within your walls.". . .
For the sake of my family and friends,
    I will say, "Peace be within you."
For the sake of the house of the LORD our God,
    I will seek your prosperity.

ISAIAH 2:3–4

The law will go out from Zion,
    the word of the LORD from Jerusalem.
He will judge between the nations
    and will settle disputes for many peoples.
They will beat their swords into plowshares
    and their spears into pruning hooks.
Nation will not take up sword against nation,
    nor will they train for war anymore.

EPHESIANS 2:14–16

For he himself is our peace, who has made the two groups one and has destroyed the barrier, the dividing wall of hostility, by setting aside in his flesh the law with its commands and regulations. His purpose was to create in himself one new humanity out of the two, thus making peace, and in one body to reconcile both of them to God through the cross.

God's peace makes friends of enemies and family of foreigners, binding together the body of Christ through His sacrifice.

God Calls Us to Make Peace

PSALM 37:10–11

A little while, and the wicked will be no more;
    though you look for them, they will not be found.
But the meek will inherit the land
    and enjoy peace and prosperity.

ISAIAH 52:7

How beautiful on the mountains
    are the feet of those who bring good news,
who proclaim peace,
    who bring good tidings,
    who proclaim salvation,
who say to Zion,
    "Your God reigns!"

MATTHEW 5:5, 8–9

Blessed are the meek,
    for they will inherit the earth. . . .
Blessed are the pure in heart,
    for they will see God.
Blessed are the peacemakers,
    for they will be called children of God.

*When have your actions or words promoted strife rather than peace?
Ask for God's forgiveness, thanking Him that He is teaching you
how to make peace.*

God Brings Peace to His People

PSALM 85:8–9

> I will listen to what God the Lord says;
> > he promises peace to his people, his faithful servants—
> > but let them not turn to folly.
> Surely his salvation is near those who fear him,
> > that his glory may dwell in our land.

DANIEL 10:18–19

Again the one who looked like a man touched me and gave me strength. "Do not be afraid, you who are highly esteemed," he said. "Peace! Be strong now; be strong."

When he spoke to me, I was strengthened and said, "Speak, my lord, since you have given me strength."

2 THESSALONIANS 3:16

Now may the Lord of peace himself give you peace at all times and in every way. The Lord be with all of you.

~~~~~~

Lord, you are the true source of peace, and you've promised peace to your people. Please give me patience as you fill me with your peace at all times and in every way.

God's Provident Care for His Creation

PSALM 145:15–16

> The eyes of all look to you,
> and you give them their food at the proper time.
> You open your hand
> and satisfy the desires of every living thing.

JOB 10:9, 12

> Remember that you molded me like clay. . . .
> You gave me life and showed me kindness,
> and in your providence watched over my spirit.

MATTHEW 6:28–30

See how the flowers of the field grow. They do not labor or spin. Yet I tell you that not even Solomon in all his splendor was dressed like one of these. If that is how God clothes the grass of the field, which is here today and tomorrow is thrown into the fire, will he not much more clothe you?

~~~~~

God's providence demonstrates His creativity, power, and care for all creation.

God's Personal Providence

PSALM 23:1–3

The LORD is my shepherd, I lack nothing.
　　He makes me lie down in green pastures,
he leads me beside quiet waters,
　　he refreshes my soul.
He guides me along the right paths
　　for his name's sake.

1 KINGS 17:4–6

"You will drink from the brook, and I have directed the ravens to supply you with food there."

So [Elijah] did what the LORD had told him. He went to the Kerith Ravine, east of the Jordan, and stayed there. The ravens brought him bread and meat in the morning and bread and meat in the evening, and he drank from the brook.

PHILIPPIANS 1:4–6

In all my prayers for all of you, I always pray with joy because of your partnership in the gospel from the first day until now, being confident of this, that he who began a good work in you will carry it on to completion until the day of Christ Jesus.

How have you recently seen God's providence in your own life? Thank Him for His generosity to you, and for carrying out His work through you.

God's Unceasing Providence

PSALM 121:1–4

I lift up my eyes to the mountains—
    where does my help come from?
My help comes from the LORD,
    the Maker of heaven and earth.

He will not let your foot slip—
    he who watches over you will not slumber;
indeed, he who watches over Israel
    will neither slumber nor sleep.

GENESIS 8:22

As long as the earth endures,
seedtime and harvest,
cold and heat,
summer and winter,
day and night
will never cease.

MARK 6:34–35, 41–42

When Jesus landed and saw a large crowd, he had compassion on them, because they were like sheep without a shepherd. So he began teaching them many things.

By this time it was late in the day. . . .

Taking the five loaves and the two fish and looking up to heaven, he gave thanks and broke the loaves. Then he gave them to his disciples to distribute to the people. He also divided the two fish among them all. They all ate and were satisfied.

~~~~~~

Lord, you are never asleep or too tired or simply unconcerned about my life. When I'm looking for help, remind me that you always watch over me.

God Provides Good from Bad

PSALM 34:8–10

Taste and see that the LORD is good;
blessed is the one who takes refuge in him.
Fear the LORD, you his holy people,
for those who fear him lack nothing.
The lions may grow weak and hungry,
but those who seek the LORD lack no good thing.

GENESIS 45:5–7

And now, do not be distressed and do not be angry with yourselves for selling me here, because it was to save lives that God sent me ahead of you. For two years now there has been famine in the land, and for the next five years there will be no plowing and reaping. But God sent me ahead of you to preserve for you a remnant on earth and to save your lives by a great deliverance.

ROMANS 8:28–29

And we know that in all things God works for the good of those who love him, who have been called according to his purpose. For those God foreknew he also predestined to be conformed to the image of his Son, that he might be the firstborn among many brothers and sisters.

Whatever hardship or brokenness you experience, God is using it to make you more like Him.

God's Providence to All Nations

PSALM 22:27–28

All the ends of the earth
>   will remember and turn to the Lord,
and all the families of the nations
>   will bow down before him,
for dominion belongs to the Lord
>   and he rules over the nations.

MALACHI 3:10, 12

"Bring the whole tithe into the storehouse, that there may be food in my house. Test me in this," says the Lord Almighty, "and see if I will not throw open the floodgates of heaven and pour out so much blessing that there will not be room enough to store it.... Then all the nations will call you blessed, for yours will be a delightful land."

ACTS 14:15–17

We are bringing you good news, telling you to turn from these worthless things to the living God, who made the heavens and the earth and the sea and everything in them. In the past, he let all nations go their own way. Yet he has not left himself without testimony: He has shown kindness by giving you rain from heaven and crops in their seasons; he provides you with plenty of food and fills your hearts with joy.

Where are you overlooking those who do not yet know God? Talk with Him, and ask Him to show you His provision and love for the nations.

God's Providence for His Covenant People

PSALM 78:23–27

Yet he gave a command to the skies above
  and opened the doors of the heavens;
he rained down manna for the people to eat,
  he gave them the grain of heaven.
Human beings ate the bread of angels;
  he sent them all the food they could eat.
He let loose the east wind from the heavens
  and by his power made the south wind blow.
He rained meat down on them like dust,
  birds like sand on the seashore.

DEUTERONOMY 8:6–9

Observe the commands of the LORD your God, walking in obedience to him and revering him. For the LORD your God is bringing you into a good land—a land with brooks, streams, and deep springs gushing out into the valleys and hills; a land with wheat and barley, vines and fig trees, pomegranates, olive oil and honey; a land where bread will not be scarce and you will lack nothing.

2 CORINTHIANS 9:8

And God is able to bless you abundantly, so that in all things at all times, having all that you need, you will abound in every good work.

~~~

Lord, thank you for your boundless provision for your people. I am so richly blessed that you've given me everything I need to do the good work of loving you, loving others, and loving your creation.

God's Providence through His Son

PSALM 22:29–31

> All the rich of the earth will feast and worship;
>> all who go down to the dust will kneel before him—
>> those who cannot keep themselves alive.
> Posterity will serve him;
>> future generations will be told about the Lord.
> They will proclaim his righteousness,
>> declaring to a people yet unborn:
>> He has done it!

GENESIS 22:13–14

Abraham looked up and there in a thicket he saw a ram caught by its horns. He went over and took the ram and sacrificed it as a burnt offering instead of his son. So Abraham called that place The Lord Will Provide. And to this day it is said, "On the mountain of the Lord it will be provided."

2 PETER 1:3–4

His divine power has given us everything we need for a godly life through our knowledge of him who called us by his own glory and goodness. Through these he has given us his very great and precious promises, so that through them you may participate in the divine nature, having escaped the corruption in the world caused by evil desires.

~~~

God provided His own Son in our place, so we can participate in the eternal life and goodness of God.

The Creator's Purposes
Prevail over All Authority

PSALM 103:17–19

But from everlasting to everlasting
the LORD's love is with those who fear him,
and his righteousness with their children's children—
with those who keep his covenant
and remember to obey his precepts.

The LORD has established his throne in heaven,
and his kingdom rules over all.

ISAIAH 14:24, 26

The LORD Almighty has sworn,

"Surely, as I have planned, so it will be,
and as I have purposed, so it will happen." . . .

This is the plan determined for the whole world;
this is the hand stretched out over all nations.

ROMANS 13:1

There is no authority except that which God has established.
The authorities that exist have been established by God.

~~~~~

*When have you seen God's purposes forwarded by someone in
authority, or accomplished despite those in authority? Pray and thank
Him that His kingdom and His plans are sure.*

The Creator's Provision
in Times of Trouble

PSALM 56:3–4

When I am afraid, I put my trust in you.
    In God, whose word I praise—
in God I trust and am not afraid.
    What can mere mortals do to me?

ESTHER 4:12–14

When Esther's words were reported to Mordecai, he sent back this answer: "Do not think that because you are in the king's house you alone of all the Jews will escape. For if you remain silent at this time, relief and deliverance for the Jews will arise from another place."

JOHN 16:31–33

"Do you now believe?" Jesus replied. "A time is coming and in fact has come when you will be scattered, each to your own home. You will leave me all alone. Yet I am not alone, for my Father is with me.

"I have told you these things, so that in me you may have peace. In this world you will have trouble. But take heart! I have overcome the world."

Lord, the world is full of trouble and pain. Please remind me to trust you when I'm afraid. Thank you for being with me, and for overcoming the world.

The Creator's Providence
When We Cannot See It

PSALM 119:114–116

You are my refuge and my shield;
    I have put my hope in your word.
Away from me, you evildoers,
    that I may keep the commands of my God!
Sustain me, my God, according to your promise, and I will live;
    do not let my hopes be dashed.

JOB 1:20–21

At this, Job got up and tore his robe and shaved his head. Then he fell to the ground in worship and said:

"Naked I came from my mother's womb,
    and naked I will depart.
The LORD gave and the LORD has taken away;
    may the name of the LORD be praised."

PHILIPPIANS 4:11–13

I am not saying this because I am in need, for I have learned to be content whatever the circumstances. I know what it is to be in need, and I know what it is to have plenty. I have learned the secret of being content in any and every situation, whether well fed or hungry, whether living in plenty or in want. I can do all this through him who gives me strength.

〜〜〜

Even when we cannot see or feel God's provision, He is the creator who is making things new.

Glorious

To God be the glory, great things He hath done;

so loved He the world that He gave us His Son,

who yielded His life an atonement for sin,

and opened the life-gate that all may go in.

Great things He hath taught us, great things
        He hath done,
and great our rejoicing through Jesus the Son;
but purer and higher and greater will be
our wonder, our transport when Jesus we see.

Praise the Lord, praise the Lord,
let the earth hear His voice!
Praise the Lord, praise the Lord,
let the people rejoice!
O come to the Father,
through Jesus the Son,
and give Him the glory,
great things He hath done.

Fanny Crosby, 1875

The God of Glory

PSALM 24:7–8

Lift up your heads, you gates;
　　be lifted up, you ancient doors,
　　that the King of glory may come in.
Who is this King of glory?
　　The Lord strong and mighty,
　　the Lord mighty in battle.

2 CHRONICLES 7:1–3

When Solomon finished praying, fire came down from heaven and consumed the burnt offering and the sacrifices, and the glory of the Lord filled the temple. The priests could not enter the temple of the Lord because the glory of the Lord filled it. When all the Israelites saw the fire coming down and the glory of the Lord above the temple, they knelt on the pavement with their faces to the ground, and they worshiped and gave thanks to the Lord, saying,

"He is good;
　　his love endures forever."

REVELATION 21:22–24

I did not see a temple in the city, because the Lord God Almighty and the Lamb are its temple. The city does not need the sun or the moon to shine on it, for the glory of God gives it light, and the Lamb is its lamp. The nations will walk by its light, and the kings of the earth will bring their splendor into it.

~~~~~~

*How are you not taking God's consuming glory seriously in your life?
Acknowledge your indifference to God, and ask Him to show you
His glory.*

The God Who Reveals His Glory

PSALM 72:18–19

Praise be to the Lord God, the God of Israel,
    who alone does marvelous deeds.
Praise be to his glorious name forever;
    may the whole earth be filled with his glory.
Amen and Amen.

ISAIAH 40:3–5

A voice of one calling:
"In the wilderness prepare
    the way for the Lord;
make straight in the desert
    a highway for our God.
Every valley shall be raised up,
    every mountain and hill made low;
the rough ground shall become level,
    the rugged places a plain.
And the glory of the Lord will be revealed,
    and all people will see it together."

LUKE 2:13–14

Suddenly a great company of the heavenly host appeared with the angel, praising God and saying,

"Glory to God in the highest heaven,
    and on earth peace to those on whom his favor rests."

~~~~~

Lord, what an awesome privilege to see your glory! Thank you for showing me yourself. Whenever I lose sight of you, please open my eyes again.

The Light of God's Glory

PSALM 76:1–4

> God is renowned in Judah;
>> in Israel his name is great.
> His tent is in Salem,
>> his dwelling place in Zion.
> There he broke the flashing arrows,
>> the shields and the swords, the weapons of war.
> You are radiant with light,
>> more majestic than mountains rich with game.

JOB 37:21–22

> Now no one can look at the sun,
>> bright as it is in the skies
>> after the wind has swept them clean.
> Out of the north he comes in golden splendor;
>> God comes in awesome majesty.

2 CORINTHIANS 4:5–6

For what we preach is not ourselves, but Jesus Christ as Lord, and ourselves as your servants for Jesus' sake. For God, who said, "Let light shine out of darkness," made his light shine in our hearts to give us the light of the knowledge of God's glory displayed in the face of Christ.

~~~~

The light of God's glory outstrips the sun—and the knowledge of His glory shines in your heart.

God's Glory over All the Earth

PSALM 57:9–11

> I will praise you, Lord, among the nations;
>> I will sing of you among the peoples.
> For great is your love, reaching to the heavens;
>> your faithfulness reaches to the skies.
>
> Be exalted, O God, above the heavens;
>> let your glory be over all the earth.

HABAKKUK 2:14

> The earth will be filled with the knowledge of the glory of the LORD as the waters cover the sea.

JOHN 17:1–3

> After Jesus said this, he looked toward heaven and prayed:
> "Father, the hour has come. Glorify your Son, that your Son may glorify you. For you granted him authority over all people that he might give eternal life to all those you have given him. Now this is eternal life: that they know you, the only true God, and Jesus Christ, whom you have sent."

Where do you see God's glory in other cultures, peoples, or places? Thank Him that His glory is everywhere, and that He is making himself known to people all over the earth.

The Glory of God's Works

PSALM 111:2–3

Great are the works of the LORD;
    they are pondered by all who delight in them.
Glorious and majestic are his deeds,
    and his righteousness endures forever.

ISAIAH 42:6–8

I, the LORD, have called you in righteousness;
    I will take hold of your hand.
I will keep you and will make you
      to be a covenant for the people
      and a light for the Gentiles,
to open eyes that are blind,
      to free captives from prison
      and to release from the dungeon those who sit in darkness.

I am the LORD; that is my name!
    I will not yield my glory to another
    or my praise to idols.

ROMANS 6:3–4

Or don't you know that all of us who were baptized into Christ Jesus were baptized into his death? We were therefore buried with him through baptism into death in order that, just as Christ was raised from the dead through the glory of the Father, we too may live a new life.

～～～

Lord, thank you for your majestic deeds: you bring righteousness, light, freedom, and new life. Your works are glorious and humbling, and I can only praise you for them.

God's Incomparable Glory

PSALM 86:8–10

> Among the gods there is none like you, Lord;
>> no deeds can compare with yours.
> All the nations you have made
>> will come and worship before you, Lord;
>> they will bring glory to your name.
> For you are great and do marvelous deeds;
>> you alone are God.

1 CHRONICLES 16:23–25

> Sing to the Lord, all the earth;
>> proclaim his salvation day after day.
> Declare his glory among the nations,
>> his marvelous deeds among all peoples.

> For great is the Lord and most worthy of praise;
>> he is to be feared above all gods.

LUKE 21:5–6, 27–28

Some of his disciples were remarking about how the temple was adorned with beautiful stones and with gifts dedicated to God. But Jesus said, "As for what you see here, the time will come when not one stone will be left on another; every one of them will be thrown down. . . .

"At that time they will see the Son of Man coming in a cloud with power and great glory. When these things begin to take place, stand up and lift up your heads, because your redemption is drawing near."

Nothing in all creation—no person, thing, or idea—can compare to the glory of the Lord.

Jesus, the Fullness of God's Glory

PSALM 63:2–4

I have seen you in the sanctuary
    and beheld your power and your glory.
Because your love is better than life,
    my lips will glorify you.
I will praise you as long as I live,
    and in your name I will lift up my hands.

EXODUS 24:15–17

When Moses went up on the mountain, the cloud covered it, and the glory of the LORD settled on Mount Sinai. For six days the cloud covered the mountain, and on the seventh day the LORD called to Moses from within the cloud. To the Israelites the glory of the LORD looked like a consuming fire on top of the mountain.

MARK 9:2–4, 7

After six days Jesus took Peter, James and John with him and led them up a high mountain, where they were all alone. There he was transfigured before them. His clothes became dazzling white, whiter than anyone in the world could bleach them. And there appeared before them Elijah and Moses, who were talking with Jesus. . . .

Then a cloud appeared and covered them, and a voice came from the cloud: "This is my Son, whom I love. Listen to him!"

When have you not listened to Jesus? Talk with Him about it, asking Him to reveal again to you who He is.

Our Omnipotent God

PSALM 66:3–4

Say to God, "How awesome are your deeds!
    So great is your power
    that your enemies cringe before you.
All the earth bows down to you;
    they sing praise to you,
    they sing the praises of your name."

JEREMIAH 32:26–27

Then the word of the LORD came to Jeremiah: "I am the LORD, the God of all mankind. Is anything too hard for me?"

MARK 10:24–27

Jesus said again, "Children, how hard it is to enter the kingdom of God! It is easier for a camel to go through the eye of a needle than for someone who is rich to enter the kingdom of God."

The disciples were even more amazed, and said to each other, "Who then can be saved?"

Jesus looked at them and said, "With man this is impossible, but not with God; all things are possible with God."

Lord, nothing is too hard for you. What is impossible for me is possible with you. Teach me to bow before you and sing your praise, resting in your complete power.

Omnipotent over All Creation

PSALM 147:15–17

> He sends his command to the earth;
>> his word runs swiftly.
> He spreads the snow like wool
>> and scatters the frost like ashes.
> He hurls down his hail like pebbles.
>> Who can withstand his icy blast?

DANIEL 2:20–22

> Praise be to the name of God for ever and ever;
>> wisdom and power are his.
> He changes times and seasons;
>> he deposes kings and raises up others. . . .
> He reveals deep and hidden things;
>> he knows what lies in darkness.

REVELATION 19:5–6

> "Praise our God,
>> all you his servants,
> you who fear him,
>> both great and small!"

Then I heard what sounded like a great multitude, like the roar of rushing waters and like loud peals of thunder, shouting:

> "Hallelujah!
> For our Lord God Almighty reigns."

In His glorious wisdom, God is all-powerful over the cycles and seasons of His creation.

Omnipotent over Human Order and Purpose

PSALM 113:7–9

He raises the poor from the dust
    and lifts the needy from the ash heap;
he seats them with princes,
    with the princes of his people.
He settles the childless woman in her home
    as a happy mother of children.
Praise the LORD.

ISAIAH 26:4–6

Trust in the LORD forever,
    for the LORD, the LORD himself, is the Rock eternal.
He humbles those who dwell on high,
    he lays the lofty city low;
he levels it to the ground
    and casts it down to the dust.
Feet trample it down—
    the feet of the oppressed,
    the footsteps of the poor.

JAMES 4:13–15

Now listen, you who say, "Today or tomorrow we will go to this or that city, spend a year there, carry on business and make money." Why, you do not even know what will happen tomorrow. What is your life? You are a mist that appears for a little while and then vanishes. Instead, you ought to say, "If it is the Lord's will, we will live and do this or that."

What word or phrase from the passages above stood out to you? Pause to talk with God about it.

Omnipotent over Life and Death

PSALM 102:19–22

> "The Lord looked down from his sanctuary on high,
>   from heaven he viewed the earth,
> to hear the groans of the prisoners
>   and release those condemned to death."
> So the name of the Lord will be declared in Zion
>   and his praise in Jerusalem
> when the peoples and the kingdoms
>   assemble to worship the Lord.

GENESIS 18:13–14

Then the Lord said to Abraham, "Why did Sarah laugh and say, 'Will I really have a child, now that I am old?' Is anything too hard for the Lord? I will return to you at the appointed time next year, and Sarah will have a son."

ACTS 26:6, 8

And now it is because of my hope in what God has promised our ancestors that I am on trial today. . . . Why should any of you consider it incredible that God raises the dead?

~~~~~~

Lord, I can't see what happens after death, or what happened before my life began. The unknown frightens me. Thank you that I don't need to try to control death because you control life and death.

Omnipotent over All Evil

PSALM 23:4

> Even though I walk
> > through the darkest valley,
> I will fear no evil,
> > for you are with me;
> your rod and your staff,
> > they comfort me.

ISAIAH 31:2–3

> Yet he too is wise and can bring disaster;
> > he does not take back his words.
> He will rise up against that wicked nation,
> > against those who help evildoers. . . .
> When the LORD stretches out his hand,
> > those who help will stumble,
> > those who are helped will fall;
> > all will perish together.

MARK 9:22–25

"If you can do anything, take pity on us and help us."

"'If you can'?" said Jesus. "Everything is possible for one who believes."

Immediately the boy's father exclaimed, "I do believe; help me overcome my unbelief!"

When Jesus saw that a crowd was running to the scene, he rebuked the impure spirit. "You deaf and mute spirit," he said, "I command you, come out of him and never enter him again."

~~~~~

Evil is a present reality in the world, but God has conquered evil, and His victory over it will be final.

Omnipotent Forever

PSALM 66:5–7

Come and see what God has done,
  his awesome deeds for mankind!
He turned the sea into dry land,
  they passed through the waters on foot—
  come, let us rejoice in him.
He rules forever by his power,
  his eyes watch the nations.

ISAIAH 50:2–3

When I came, why was there no one?
  When I called, why was there no one to answer?
Was my arm too short to deliver you?
  Do I lack the strength to rescue you?
By a mere rebuke I dry up the sea,
  I turn rivers into a desert;
their fish rot for lack of water
  and die of thirst.
I clothe the heavens with darkness
  and make sackcloth its covering.

JUDE 24–25

To him who is able to keep you from stumbling and to present you before his glorious presence without fault and with great joy—to the only God our Savior be glory, majesty, power and authority, through Jesus Christ our Lord, before all ages, now and forevermore! Amen.

In what area of your life are you not trusting God's power? Bring your questions to Him, praying that He gently remind you of His ability to keep you always and present you faultless in the end.

Jesus, the Omnipotent God Revealed

PSALM 136:23–24

> He remembered us in our low estate
> > *His love endures forever.*
> and freed us from our enemies.
> > *His love endures forever.*

AMOS 4:12–13

> "Therefore this is what I will do to you, Israel,
> > and because I will do this to you, Israel,
> > prepare to meet your God."

> He who forms the mountains,
> > who creates the wind,
> > and who reveals his thoughts to mankind,
> who turns dawn to darkness,
> > and treads on the heights of the earth—
> > the Lord God Almighty is his name.

MARK 4:37–39, 41

> The waves broke over the boat, so that it was nearly swamped. Jesus was in the stern, sleeping on a cushion. The disciples woke him and said to him, "Teacher, don't you care if we drown?"
>
> He got up, rebuked the wind and said to the waves, "Quiet! Be still!" Then the wind died down and it was completely calm. . . .
>
> They were terrified and asked each other, "Who is this? Even the wind and the waves obey him!"

~~~~~~~~

Lord, thank you for bringing the fullness of yourself to earth in the person of Jesus. Your power over all things amazes me. I want to meet with you and know you as you are.

The Sovereign Lord

PSALM 71:15–16

My mouth will tell of your righteous deeds,
> of your saving acts all day long—
> though I know not how to relate them all.
I will come and proclaim your mighty acts, Sovereign LORD;
> I will proclaim your righteous deeds, yours alone.

DANIEL 4:17

The decision is announced by messengers, the holy ones declare the verdict, so that the living may know that the Most High is sovereign over all kingdoms on earth and gives them to anyone he wishes and sets over them the lowliest of people.

ACTS 5:38–39

Therefore, in the present case I advise you: Leave these men alone! Let them go! For if their purpose or activity is of human origin, it will fail. But if it is from God, you will not be able to stop these men; you will only find yourselves fighting against God.

~~~

God is sovereign over everything in all creation. What is from God will be.

God's Sovereignty
over Every Circumstance

PSALM 71:5–6

For you have been my hope, Sovereign LORD,
    my confidence since my youth.
From birth I have relied on you;
    you brought me forth from my mother's womb.
    I will ever praise you.

JOB 12:14–16

What he tears down cannot be rebuilt;
    those he imprisons cannot be released.
If he holds back the waters, there is drought;
    if he lets them loose, they devastate the land.
To him belong strength and insight;
    both deceived and deceiver are his.

LUKE 12:6–7

Are not five sparrows sold for two pennies? Yet not one of them is
forgotten by God. Indeed, the very hairs of your head are all numbered.
Don't be afraid; you are worth more than many sparrows.

*Where have you recently seen God's sovereignty in the details of
your life? Thank Him for His care, and for His complete knowledge
of you.*

God's Sovereignty amid Hardship

PSALM 109:21–22

But you, Sovereign LORD,
    help me for your name's sake;
    out of the goodness of your love, deliver me.
For I am poor and needy,
    and my heart is wounded within me.

ECCLESIASTES 7:13–14

Consider what God has done:

Who can straighten
    what he has made crooked?
When times are good, be happy;
    but when times are bad, consider this:
God has made the one
    as well as the other.
Therefore, no one can discover
    anything about their future.

PHILIPPIANS 2:12–15

Therefore, my dear friends, as you have always obeyed—not only in my presence, but now much more in my absence—continue to work out your salvation with fear and trembling, for it is God who works in you to will and to act in order to fulfill his good purpose. Do everything without grumbling or arguing, so that you may become blameless and pure, "children of God without fault in a warped and crooked generation."

~~~~~

Lord, I don't understand why you've made times that are bad, or how you're still sovereign when my heart is hurt. Please teach me to trust you, knowing that you are making me like you.

God's Sovereignty over Death

PSALM 68:19–20

Praise be to the LORD, to God our Savior,
    who daily bears our burdens.
Our God is a God who saves;
    from the Sovereign LORD comes escape from death.

ISAIAH 25:7–8

On this mountain he will destroy
    the shroud that enfolds all peoples,
the sheet that covers all nations;
    he will swallow up death forever.
The Sovereign LORD will wipe away the tears
    from all faces;
he will remove his people's disgrace
    from all the earth.
    The LORD has spoken.

COLOSSIANS 1:18–20

He is the head of the body, the church; he is the beginning and the firstborn from among the dead, so that in everything he might have the supremacy. For God was pleased to have all his fullness dwell in him, and through him to reconcile to himself all things, whether things on earth or things in heaven, by making peace through his blood, shed on the cross.

~~~~~

God has the power to swallow up death forever. Jesus is the firstborn from the dead, and all who follow Him will also rise from the dead.

God's Sovereignty
over Human Rebellion

PSALM 73:27–28

> Those who are far from you will perish;
>> you destroy all who are unfaithful to you.
> But as for me, it is good to be near God.
>> I have made the Sovereign LORD my refuge;
>> I will tell of all your deeds.

GENESIS 50:19–20

But Joseph said to them, "Don't be afraid. Am I in the place of God? You intended to harm me, but God intended it for good to accomplish what is now being done, the saving of many lives."

ACTS 4:27–29

Indeed Herod and Pontius Pilate met together with the Gentiles and the people of Israel in this city to conspire against your holy servant Jesus, whom you anointed. They did what your power and will had decided beforehand should happen. Now, Lord, consider their threats and enable your servants to speak your word with great boldness.

When have you knowingly rebelled against God? Confess to Him, and thank Him that He is sovereign even over those who are not seeking His will.

God's Sovereignty
over All Authority

PSALM 104:10–13

He makes springs pour water into the ravines;
    it flows between the mountains.
They give water to all the beasts of the field;
    the wild donkeys quench their thirst.
The birds of the sky nest by the waters;
    they sing among the branches.
He waters the mountains from his upper chambers;
    the land is satisfied by the fruit of his work.

JEREMIAH 27:4–5

This is what the LORD Almighty, the God of Israel, says: "Tell this
to your masters: With my great power and outstretched arm I made the
earth and its people and the animals that are on it, and I give it to anyone
I please."

JOHN 19:8–11

"Where do you come from?" he asked Jesus, but Jesus gave him no
answer. "Do you refuse to speak to me?" Pilate said. "Don't you realize I
have power either to free you or to crucify you?"

Jesus answered, "You would have no power over me if it were not
given to you from above. Therefore the one who handed me over to you
is guilty of a greater sin."

~~~~~

*Lord, there is no human rule or authority that is outside of your
sovereignty. Even when people misuse their power, remind me that
you see everything and are in control.*

The Glory of God's Sovereignty

PSALM 29:7–9

> The voice of the LORD strikes
>> with flashes of lightning.
> The voice of the LORD shakes the desert;
>> the LORD shakes the Desert of Kadesh.
> The voice of the LORD twists the oaks
>> and strips the forests bare.
> And in his temple all cry, "Glory!"

1 CHRONICLES 29:12–13

> You are the ruler of all things.
> In your hands are strength and power
>> to exalt and give strength to all.
> Now, our God, we give you thanks,
>> and praise your glorious name.

REVELATION 1:12–16

When I turned I saw seven golden lampstands, and among the lampstands was someone like a son of man, dressed in a robe reaching down to his feet and with a golden sash around his chest. The hair on his head was white like wool, as white as snow, and his eyes were like blazing fire. His feet were like bronze glowing in a furnace, and his voice was like the sound of rushing waters. In his right hand he held seven stars, and coming out of his mouth was a sharp, double-edged sword. His face was like the sun shining in all its brilliance.

God rules over all things, and His glory is more powerful and overwhelming than anything in creation He could be compared to.

The Beauty of the Lord

PSALM 27:4

> One thing I ask from the LORD,
>   this only do I seek:
> that I may dwell in the house of the LORD
>   all the days of my life,
> to gaze on the beauty of the LORD
>   and to seek him in his temple.

ISAIAH 28:5–6

> In that day the LORD Almighty
>   will be a glorious crown,
> a beautiful wreath
>   for the remnant of his people.
> He will be a spirit of justice
>   to the one who sits in judgment,
> a source of strength
>   to those who turn back the battle at the gate.

2 CORINTHIANS 4:4

The god of this age has blinded the minds of unbelievers, so that they cannot see the light of the gospel that displays the glory of Christ, who is the image of God.

~~~

What do you find beautiful about God? Share this with Him, praising Him for what you see in Him.

The Beauty of God's Glory

PSALM 34:4–5

I sought the LORD, and he answered me;
    he delivered me from all my fears.
Those who look to him are radiant;
    their faces are never covered with shame.

EXODUS 34:28–30

Moses was there with the LORD forty days and forty nights without eating bread or drinking water. And he wrote on the tablets the words of the covenant—the Ten Commandments.

When Moses came down from Mount Sinai with the two tablets of the covenant law in his hands, he was not aware that his face was radiant because he had spoken with the LORD. When Aaron and all the Israelites saw Moses, his face was radiant, and they were afraid to come near him.

2 PETER 1:16–18

For we did not follow cleverly devised stories when we told you about the coming of our Lord Jesus Christ in power, but we were eyewitnesses of his majesty. He received honor and glory from God the Father when the voice came to him from the Majestic Glory, saying, "This is my Son, whom I love; with him I am well pleased." We ourselves heard this voice that came from heaven when we were with him on the sacred mountain.

~~~~~

Lord, your glory is so strong, even those who see your face reflect its radiance. Thank you for sharing your beauty with me. I want to see you face-to-face.

The Beauty of God's Presence among His People

PSALM 48:1–3

> Great is the LORD, and most worthy of praise,
>> in the city of our God, his holy mountain.
>
> Beautiful in its loftiness,
>> the joy of the whole earth,
> like the heights of Zaphon is Mount Zion,
>> the city of the Great King.
> God is in her citadels;
>> he has shown himself to be her fortress.

NUMBERS 24:5–7

> How beautiful are your tents, Jacob,
>> your dwelling places, Israel!
>
> Like valleys they spread out,
>> like gardens beside a river,
> like aloes planted by the LORD,
>> like cedars beside the waters.
> Water will flow from their buckets;
>> their seed will have abundant water.

REVELATION 21:10–11

He carried me away in the Spirit to a mountain great and high, and showed me the Holy City, Jerusalem, coming down out of heaven from God. It shone with the glory of God, and its brilliance was like that of a very precious jewel, like a jasper, clear as crystal.

~~~

God's glorious beauty shines through the body of Christ—the temple where His Spirit dwells.

The Beauty of God's Works

PSALM 90:16

> May your deeds be shown to your servants,
> your splendor to their children.

ZECHARIAH 9:16–17

> The LORD their God will save his people on that day
> as a shepherd saves his flock.
> They will sparkle in his land
> like jewels in a crown.
> How attractive and beautiful they will be!
> Grain will make the young men thrive,
> and new wine the young women.

PHILIPPIANS 4:8

> Finally, brothers and sisters, whatever is true, whatever is noble, whatever is right, whatever is pure, whatever is lovely, whatever is admirable—if anything is excellent or praiseworthy—think about such things.

Where are you dwelling on the challenging, difficult, or harmful things in life? Talk with Him about what you're feeling. Ask Him to remind you gently, when you need it, of the beauty of His works.

Godly Inner Beauty

PSALM 139:23–24

> Search me, God, and know my heart;
>   test me and know my anxious thoughts.
> See if there is any offensive way in me,
>   and lead me in the way everlasting.

1 SAMUEL 16:6–7

When they arrived, Samuel saw Eliab and thought, "Surely the Lord's anointed stands here before the Lord."

But the Lord said to Samuel, "Do not consider his appearance or his height, for I have rejected him. The Lord does not look at the things people look at. People look at the outward appearance, but the Lord looks at the heart."

1 PETER 3:3–4

Your beauty should not come from outward adornment. . . . Rather, it should be that of your inner self, the unfading beauty of a gentle and quiet spirit, which is of great worth in God's sight.

～～～

Lord, thank you that your beauty shines from your good and loving character. It's not a matter of social influence or expensive clothes or products. I want to be beautiful the way you're beautiful.

The Beauty of God's Wisdom

PSALM 73:23–24

> Yet I am always with you;
>> you hold me by my right hand.
> You guide me with your counsel,
>> and afterward you will take me into glory.

PROVERBS 3:13–18

> Blessed are those who find wisdom,
>> those who gain understanding,
> for she is more profitable than silver
>> and yields better returns than gold.
> She is more precious than rubies;
>> nothing you desire can compare with her.
> Long life is in her right hand;
>> in her left hand are riches and honor.
> Her ways are pleasant ways,
>> and all her paths are peace.
> She is a tree of life to those who take hold of her;
>> those who hold her fast will be blessed.

EPHESIANS 1:17

I keep asking that the God of our Lord Jesus Christ, the glorious Father, may give you the Spirit of wisdom and revelation, so that you may know him better.

~~~~~~

God's wisdom guides His children, exhibiting His glory and beauty, that you may know Him better.

The Beauty of God's Restoration

PSALM 50:2

From Zion, perfect in beauty,
God shines forth.

ISAIAH 4:2–3, 5

In that day the Branch of the LORD will be beautiful and glorious, and the fruit of the land will be the pride and glory of the survivors in Israel. Those who are left in Zion, who remain in Jerusalem, will be called holy, all who are recorded among the living in Jerusalem. . . . Then the LORD will create over all of Mount Zion and over those who assemble there a cloud of smoke by day and a glow of flaming fire by night; over everything the glory will be a canopy.

TITUS 2:10–12

In every way they will make the teaching about God our Savior attractive.

For the grace of God has appeared that offers salvation to all people. It teaches us to say "No" to ungodliness and worldly passions, and to live self-controlled, upright and godly lives in this present age.

~~~~

When was a time you saw the beauty of God reflected in His people? Ask God to teach you to be self-controlled, upright, and godly, so you can help attract others to His beautiful salvation.

The Glory Due His Name

PSALM 96:7–8

> Ascribe to the LORD, all you families of nations,
>> ascribe to the LORD glory and strength.
> Ascribe to the LORD the glory due his name;
>> bring an offering and come into his courts.

1 CHRONICLES 16:31–33

> Let the heavens rejoice, let the earth be glad;
>> let them say among the nations, "The LORD reigns!"
> Let the sea resound, and all that is in it;
>> let the fields be jubilant, and everything in them!
> Let the trees of the forest sing,
>> let them sing for joy before the LORD,
>> for he comes to judge the earth.

1 CORINTHIANS 10:31

> So whether you eat or drink or whatever you do, do it all for the glory of God.

～～

Lord, you deserve all the praise and thanksgiving your people could ever give you. Even the seas and fields and forests praise you! Teach me to do everything I do as an act of worship to you.

God's Glory Far above Humanity

PSALM 115:1

Not to us, LORD, not to us
    but to your name be the glory,
    because of your love and faithfulness.

ISAIAH 45:9–10

Woe to those who quarrel with their Maker,
    those who are nothing but potsherds
    among the potsherds on the ground.
Does the clay say to the potter,
    "What are you making?"
Does your work say,
    "The potter has no hands"?
Woe to the one who says to a father,
    "What have you begotten?"
or to a mother,
    "What have you brought to birth?"

LUKE 1:51–53

He has performed mighty deeds with his arm;
    he has scattered those who are proud in their inmost thoughts.
He has brought down rulers from their thrones
    but has lifted up the humble.
He has filled the hungry with good things
    but has sent the rich away empty.

~~~~~~

*God's glory—His might, sovereignty, love, and faithfulness—far
outstrips any human prestige.*

Beholding the Glory of God

PSALM 102:15–17

The nations will fear the name of the LORD,
 all the kings of the earth will revere your glory.
For the LORD will rebuild Zion
 and appear in his glory.
He will respond to the prayer of the destitute;
 he will not despise their plea.

DEUTERONOMY 5:23–24

When you heard the voice out of the darkness, while the mountain was ablaze with fire, all the leaders of your tribes and your elders came to me. And you said, "The LORD our God has shown us his glory and his majesty, and we have heard his voice from the fire. Today we have seen that a person can live even if God speaks with them."

1 JOHN 1:1–2

That which was from the beginning, which we have heard, which we have seen with our eyes, which we have looked at and our hands have touched—this we proclaim concerning the Word of life. The life appeared; we have seen it and testify to it, and we proclaim to you the eternal life, which was with the Father and has appeared to us.

Where in your life do you feel like you aren't seeing God's glory? Pray, thanking Him that He is a God who reveals himself, and that He came in the flesh to be seen and heard and touched.

Just

What can wash away my sin?

Nothing but the blood of Jesus.

What can make me whole again?

Nothing but the blood of Jesus.

For my pardon this I see:
nothing but the blood of Jesus.
For my cleansing this my plea:
nothing but the blood of Jesus.

Nothing can for sin atone:
nothing but the blood of Jesus.
Naught of good that I have done:
nothing but the blood of Jesus.

This is all my hope and peace:
nothing but the blood of Jesus.
This is all my righteousness:
nothing but the blood of Jesus.

O precious is the flow
that makes me white as snow;
no other fount I know;
nothing but the blood of Jesus.

Robert Lowry, 1876

The God of Justice

PSALM 99:4–5

> The King is mighty, he loves justice—
> you have established equity;
> in Jacob you have done
> what is just and right.
> Exalt the LORD our God
> and worship at his footstool;
> he is holy.

JEREMIAH 9:23–24

> "Let not the wise boast of their wisdom
> or the strong boast of their strength
> or the rich boast of their riches,
> but let the one who boasts boast about this:
> that they have the understanding to know me,
> that I am the LORD, who exercises kindness,
> justice and righteousness on earth,
> for in these I delight,"
> declares the LORD.

LUKE 18:6–8

And the Lord said, "Listen to what the unjust judge says. And will not God bring about justice for his chosen ones, who cry out to him day and night? Will he keep putting them off? I tell you, he will see that they get justice, and quickly."

~~~

Lord, you love justice—right and equitable relationships between all the people you've made. Thank you for being a righteous and kind King as you bring your justice on earth.

God's Justice for Those in Need

PSALM 140:12–13

> I know that the LORD secures justice for the poor
>   and upholds the cause of the needy.
> Surely the righteous will praise your name,
>   and the upright will live in your presence.

RUTH 2:11–12

Boaz replied, "I've been told all about what you have done for your mother-in-law since the death of your husband—how you left your father and mother and your homeland and came to live with a people you did not know before. May the LORD repay you for what you have done. May you be richly rewarded by the LORD, the God of Israel, under whose wings you have come to take refuge."

JAMES 1:26–27

Those who consider themselves religious and yet do not keep a tight rein on their tongues deceive themselves, and their religion is worthless. Religion that God our Father accepts as pure and faultless is this: to look after orphans and widows in their distress and to keep oneself from being polluted by the world.

~~~~~

God desires justice for the poor and needy, the orphans and widows. He calls you to seek justice for them too.

God's Justice When the World Is Unjust

PSALM 82:2–4

How long will you defend the unjust
  and show partiality to the wicked?
Defend the weak and the fatherless;
  uphold the cause of the poor and the oppressed.
Rescue the weak and the needy;
  deliver them from the hand of the wicked.

ECCLESIASTES 5:8–10

If you see the poor oppressed in a district, and justice and rights denied, do not be surprised at such things; for one official is eyed by a higher one, and over them both are others higher still. The increase from the land is taken by all; the king himself profits from the fields.

Whoever loves money never has enough;
  whoever loves wealth is never satisfied with their income.
  This too is meaningless.

REVELATION 6:9–10

When he opened the fifth seal, I saw under the altar the souls of those who had been slain because of the word of God and the testimony they had maintained. They called out in a loud voice, "How long, Sovereign Lord, holy and true, until you judge the inhabitants of the earth and avenge our blood?"

～～～

Have you witnessed a situation where justice came after a painful time of injustice? Thank God that He is bringing His justice to the earth, and ask Him for patient endurance as you wait and work.

God Desires Justice, Not Sacrifice

PSALM 50:6–8

The heavens proclaim his righteousness,
   for he is a God of justice.

"Listen, my people, and I will speak;
   I will testify against you, Israel:
   I am God, your God.
I bring no charges against you concerning your sacrifices
   or concerning your burnt offerings, which are ever before me."

AMOS 5:22–24

Even though you bring me burnt offerings and grain offerings,
   I will not accept them.
Though you bring choice fellowship offerings,
   I will have no regard for them.
Away with the noise of your songs!
   I will not listen to the music of your harps.
But let justice roll on like a river,
   righteousness like a never-failing stream!

LUKE 11:42

Woe to you Pharisees, because you give God a tenth of your mint, rue and all other kinds of garden herbs, but you neglect justice and the love of God. You should have practiced the latter without leaving the former undone.

Lord, too often I think you just want my money or my possessions, my prayers and my worship songs. Forgive me. Please teach me your justice, your active care for my fellow image bearers you love.

God's Disciplining Justice

PSALM 58:9, 11

Before your pots can feel the heat of the thorns—
    whether they be green or dry—the wicked will be swept away. . . .
Then people will say,
    "Surely the righteous still are rewarded;
    surely there is a God who judges the earth."

ISAIAH 10:1–3

Woe to those who make unjust laws,
    to those who issue oppressive decrees,
to deprive the poor of their rights
    and withhold justice from the oppressed of my people,
making widows their prey
    and robbing the fatherless.
What will you do on the day of reckoning,
    when disaster comes from afar?
To whom will you run for help?
    Where will you leave your riches?

GALATIANS 6:7–8

Do not be deceived: God cannot be mocked. A man reaps what
he sows. Whoever sows to please their flesh, from the flesh will reap
destruction; whoever sows to please the Spirit, from the Spirit will reap
eternal life.

*God corrects injustice and oppression—and that includes painful
reckoning for sin.*

God's Unfailing Justice

PSALM 37:27–28

> Turn from evil and do good;
>> then you will dwell in the land forever.
> For the LORD loves the just
>> and will not forsake his faithful ones.

ZEPHANIAH 3:5

> The LORD within her is righteous;
>> he does no wrong.
> Morning by morning he dispenses his justice,
>> and every new day he does not fail.

MATTHEW 12:15–18, 20

A large crowd followed [Jesus], and he healed all who were ill. He warned them not to tell others about him. This was to fulfill what was spoken through the prophet Isaiah:

> "Here is my servant whom I have chosen,
>> the one I love, in whom I delight;
>
> I will put my Spirit on him,
>> and he will proclaim justice to the nations. . . .
>
> A bruised reed he will not break,
>> and a smoldering wick he will not snuff out,
>> till he has brought justice through to victory."

Where do you see injustice prevailing in the world today? Mourn with God about it. Thank Him that He is bringing a new day of justice, and that He will not fail.

The Justice of God's Redemption

PSALM 33:5

> The LORD loves righteousness and justice;
> the earth is full of his unfailing love.

ISAIAH 51:4–5

> Listen to me, my people;
> hear me, my nation:
> Instruction will go out from me;
> my justice will become a light to the nations.
> My righteousness draws near speedily,
> my salvation is on the way,
> and my arm will bring justice to the nations.
> The islands will look to me
> and wait in hope for my arm.

ROMANS 3:21–24

But now apart from the law the righteousness of God has been made known, to which the Law and the Prophets testify. This righteousness is given through faith in Jesus Christ to all who believe. There is no difference between Jew and Gentile, for all have sinned and fall short of the glory of God, and all are justified freely by his grace through the redemption that came by Christ Jesus.

~~~

Lord, you have dealt justly with my sins—through the free gift of Jesus's death and resurrection. Thank you for righting my wrongs, restoring our relationship, and loving me without fail.

The Righteousness of God

PSALM 89:14–15

Righteousness and justice are the foundation of your throne;
  love and faithfulness go before you.
Blessed are those who have learned to acclaim you,
  who walk in the light of your presence, LORD.

JOB 37:23–24

The Almighty is beyond our reach and exalted in power;
  in his justice and great righteousness, he does not oppress.
Therefore, people revere him,
  for does he not have regard for all the wise in heart?

ROMANS 1:16–17

For I am not ashamed of the gospel, because it is the power of God that brings salvation to everyone who believes: first to the Jew, then to the Gentile. For in the gospel the righteousness of God is revealed—a righteousness that is by faith from first to last, just as it is written: "The righteous will live by faith."

God does right by everyone and everything.

God's Everlasting Righteousness

PSALM 119:142–144

> Your righteousness is everlasting
>   and your law is true.
> Trouble and distress have come upon me,
>   but your commands give me delight.
> Your statutes are always righteous;
>   give me understanding that I may live.

DANIEL 9:24

Seventy "sevens" are decreed for your people and your holy city to finish transgression, to put an end to sin, to atone for wickedness, to bring in everlasting righteousness, to seal up vision and prophecy and to anoint the Most Holy Place.

PHILIPPIANS 1:9–11

And this is my prayer: that your love may abound more and more in knowledge and depth of insight, so that you may be able to discern what is best and may be pure and blameless for the day of Christ, filled with the fruit of righteousness that comes through Jesus Christ—to the glory and praise of God.

~~~~~

What word or phrase from the passages above stood out to you?
Pause to talk with God about it.

The Righteousness of God's Commands

PSALM 119:137–138

> You are righteous, LORD,
>   and your laws are right.
> The statutes you have laid down are righteous;
>   they are fully trustworthy.

ISAIAH 56:1–2

> This is what the LORD says:

> "Maintain justice
>   and do what is right,
> for my salvation is close at hand
>   and my righteousness will soon be revealed.
> Blessed is the one who does this—
>   the person who holds it fast,
> who keeps the Sabbath without desecrating it,
>   and keeps their hands from doing any evil."

1 JOHN 2:28–29

And now, dear children, continue in him, so that when he appears we may be confident and unashamed before him at his coming.

If you know that he is righteous, you know that everyone who does what is right has been born of him.

～～～

Lord, thank you for your commands, which show me how to maintain justice and keep my hands from evil. Please continue teaching me to live out your law, doing right in all my relationships.

God's Righteousness
to His Covenant People

PSALM 48:9–11

Within your temple, O God,
  we meditate on your unfailing love.
Like your name, O God,
  your praise reaches to the ends of the earth;
  your right hand is filled with righteousness.
Mount Zion rejoices,
  the villages of Judah are glad
  because of your judgments.

1 SAMUEL 12:6–7

Then Samuel said to the people, "It is the Lord who appointed Moses and Aaron and brought your ancestors up out of Egypt. Now then, stand here, because I am going to confront you with evidence before the Lord as to all the righteous acts performed by the Lord for you and your ancestors."

ROMANS 10:1–4

My heart's desire and prayer to God for the Israelites is that they may be saved. For I can testify about them that they are zealous for God, but their zeal is not based on knowledge. Since they did not know the righteousness of God and sought to establish their own, they did not submit to God's righteousness. Christ is the culmination of the law so that there may be righteousness for everyone who believes.

〜〜

God has always done right for His people—and He will continue to through the righteousness of Jesus.

God's Righteous Judgment

PSALM 96:12–13

> Let the fields be jubilant, and everything in them;
>> let all the trees of the forest sing for joy.
> Let all creation rejoice before the LORD, for he comes,
>> he comes to judge the earth.
> He will judge the world in righteousness
>> and the peoples in his faithfulness.

EZRA 9:13, 15

What has happened to us is a result of our evil deeds and our great guilt, and yet, our God, you have punished us less than our sins deserved and have given us a remnant like this. . . . LORD, the God of Israel, you are righteous! We are left this day as a remnant. Here we are before you in our guilt, though because of it not one of us can stand in your presence.

EPHESIANS 4:22–24

You were taught, with regard to your former way of life, to put off your old self, which is being corrupted by its deceitful desires; to be made new in the attitude of your minds; and to put on the new self, created to be like God in true righteousness and holiness.

~

Does God's judgment feel like He is wronging you? Talk openly with Him about it. Ask Him to show you how He is treating you righteously, and how He is renewing you to be righteous too.

God's Righteousness and Faith

PSALM 71:19

> Your righteousness, God, reaches to the heavens,
> you who have done great things.
> Who is like you, God?

GENESIS 15:5–6

[The Lord] took [Abram] outside and said, "Look up at the sky and count the stars—if indeed you can count them." Then he said to him, "So shall your offspring be."

Abram believed the LORD, and he credited it to him as righteousness.

JAMES 2:22–24

You see that his faith and his actions were working together, and his faith was made complete by what he did. And the scripture was fulfilled that says, "Abraham believed God, and it was credited to him as righteousness," and he was called God's friend. You see that a person is considered righteous by what they do and not by faith alone.

Lord, help my unbelief when your promises sound impossible. Thank you that believing you is itself a righteous act. Our friendship is right when I trust you and your infinite ability.

The Righteousness of Jesus

PSALM 40:9–10

> I proclaim your saving acts in the great assembly;
>> I do not seal my lips, Lord,
>> as you know.
> I do not hide your righteousness in my heart;
>> I speak of your faithfulness and your saving help.

ISAIAH 53:10–11

> Yet it was the Lord's will to crush him and cause him to suffer,
>> and though the Lord makes his life an offering for sin,
> he will see his offspring and prolong his days,
>> and the will of the Lord will prosper in his hand.
> After he has suffered,
>> he will see the light of life and be satisfied;
> by his knowledge my righteous servant will justify many,
>> and he will bear their iniquities.

1 PETER 2:24–25

"He himself bore our sins" in his body on the cross, so that we might die to sins and live for righteousness; "by his wounds you have been healed." For "you were like sheep going astray," but now you have returned to the Shepherd and Overseer of your souls.

~~~

Jesus did right in His sacrificial death despite human wrongdoing, restoring right relationship with His creation.

Our Immutable God

PSALM 55:19

> God, who is enthroned from of old,
>> who does not change—
> he will hear them and humble them,
>> because they have no fear of God.

NUMBERS 23:19–20

> God is not human, that he should lie,
>> not a human being, that he should change his mind.
> Does he speak and then not act?
>> Does he promise and not fulfill?
> I have received a command to bless;
>> he has blessed, and I cannot change it.

JAMES 1:17–18

Every good and perfect gift is from above, coming down from the Father of the heavenly lights, who does not change like shifting shadows. He chose to give us birth through the word of truth, that we might be a kind of firstfruits of all he created.

~~~~

How have you seen God's justice, faithfulness, or love in the past? Praise Him for what He has done, and thank Him that He is the same today.

God's Immutable Word

PSALM 119:89–91

> Your word, LORD, is eternal;
>   it stands firm in the heavens.
> Your faithfulness continues through all generations;
>   you established the earth, and it endures.
> Your laws endure to this day,
>   for all things serve you.

ISAIAH 46:11

> From the east I summon a bird of prey;
>   from a far-off land, a man to fulfill my purpose.
> What I have said, that I will bring about;
>   what I have planned, that I will do.

2 PETER 1:19–21

We also have the prophetic message as something completely reliable, and you will do well to pay attention to it, as to a light shining in a dark place, until the day dawns and the morning star rises in your hearts. Above all, you must understand that no prophecy of Scripture came about by the prophet's own interpretation of things. For prophecy never had its origin in the human will, but prophets, though human, spoke from God as they were carried along by the Holy Spirit.

Lord, I'm grateful your word is unchanging. What you've said you'll do, you'll do. Please deepen my trust: I know you are completely reliable.

God's Immutable Promises

PSALM 59:9–10

> You are my strength, I watch for you;
> > you, God, are my fortress,
> > my God on whom I can rely.

EXODUS 32:11–14

But Moses sought the favor of the LORD his God. . . . "Turn from your fierce anger; relent and do not bring disaster on your people. Remember your servants Abraham, Isaac and Israel, to whom you swore by your own self: 'I will make your descendants as numerous as the stars in the sky and I will give your descendants all this land I promised them, and it will be their inheritance forever.'" Then the LORD relented and did not bring on his people the disaster he had threatened.

HEBREWS 6:13–15, 17

When God made his promise to Abraham, since there was no one greater for him to swear by, he swore by himself, saying, "I will surely bless you and give you many descendants." And so after waiting patiently, Abraham received what was promised. . . .

Because God wanted to make the unchanging nature of his purpose very clear to the heirs of what was promised, he confirmed it with an oath.

~~~~~

Every promise of God will come to pass.

God's Immutable Justice

PSALM 20:6–8

Now this I know:
  The Lord gives victory to his anointed.
He answers him from his heavenly sanctuary
  with the victorious power of his right hand.
Some trust in chariots and some in horses,
  but we trust in the name of the Lord our God.
They are brought to their knees and fall,
  but we rise up and stand firm.

EZEKIEL 24:14

I the Lord have spoken. The time has come for me to act. I will not hold back; I will not have pity, nor will I relent. You will be judged according to your conduct and your actions, declares the Sovereign Lord.

ACTS 17:31

For he has set a day when he will judge the world with justice by the man he has appointed. He has given proof of this to everyone by raising him from the dead.

~~~

Where would you rather avoid God's justice? Be honest with Him. Thank Him that Jesus is both trustworthy and life-giving in His judgments.

God's Immutable Mercy

PSALM 71:1–3

> In you, LORD, I have taken refuge;
>> let me never be put to shame.
> In your righteousness, rescue me and deliver me;
>> turn your ear to me and save me.
> Be my rock of refuge,
>> to which I can always go;
> give the command to save me,
>> for you are my rock and my fortress.

MALACHI 3:6–7

"I the LORD do not change. So you, the descendants of Jacob, are not destroyed. Ever since the time of your ancestors you have turned away from my decrees and have not kept them. Return to me, and I will return to you," says the LORD Almighty.

ROMANS 11:28–31

As far as the gospel is concerned, they are enemies for your sake; but as far as election is concerned, they are loved on account of the patriarchs, for God's gifts and his call are irrevocable. Just as you who were at one time disobedient to God have now received mercy as a result of their disobedience, so they too have now become disobedient in order that they too may now receive mercy as a result of God's mercy to you.

Lord, thank you that your mercy is an essential part of your justice and righteousness; it's part of how you right wrongs and bring about reconciliation. I'm so glad that you do not change.

God's Immutable Purposes

PSALM 71:17–18

Since my youth, God, you have taught me,
    and to this day I declare your marvelous deeds.
Even when I am old and gray,
    do not forsake me, my God,
till I declare your power to the next generation,
    your mighty acts to all who are to come.

PROVERBS 19:21

Many are the plans in a person's heart,
    but it is the LORD's purpose that prevails.

ACTS 2:22–24

Fellow Israelites, listen to this: Jesus of Nazareth was a man accredited by God to you by miracles, wonders and signs, which God did among you through him, as you yourselves know. This man was handed over to you by God's deliberate plan and foreknowledge; and you, with the help of wicked men, put him to death by nailing him to the cross. But God raised him from the dead, freeing him from the agony of death, because it was impossible for death to keep its hold on him.

~~~

Yesterday, today, and tomorrow, God is working out His purposes—even when you aren't sure how.

God's Immutable Love

PSALM 21:7

> For the king trusts in the LORD;
>> through the unfailing love of the Most High
>> he will not be shaken.

JEREMIAH 31:3–4

The LORD appeared to us in the past, saying:

> "I have loved you with an everlasting love;
>> I have drawn you with unfailing kindness.
> I will build you up again,
>> and you, Virgin Israel, will be rebuilt.
> Again you will take up your timbrels
>> and go out to dance with the joyful."

ROMANS 8:38–39

For I am convinced that neither death nor life, neither angels nor demons, neither the present nor the future, nor any powers, neither height nor depth, nor anything else in all creation, will be able to separate us from the love of God that is in Christ Jesus our Lord.

What evidence of God's love do you see in your life today? Thank Him for His unfailing love, and ask Him for an ever-deepening awareness of His love.

The Wrath of God

PSALM 2:9–12

"You will break them with a rod of iron;
    you will dash them to pieces like pottery."

Therefore, you kings, be wise;
    be warned, you rulers of the earth.
Serve the Lord with fear
    and celebrate his rule with trembling.
Kiss his son, or he will be angry
    and your way will lead to your destruction,
for his wrath can flare up in a moment.
    Blessed are all who take refuge in him.

NAHUM 1:2, 6

The Lord takes vengeance on his foes
    and vents his wrath against his enemies. . . .
Who can withstand his indignation?
    Who can endure his fierce anger?
His wrath is poured out like fire;
    the rocks are shattered before him.

REVELATION 19:13, 15

He is dressed in a robe dipped in blood, and his name is the Word of God. . . . Coming out of his mouth is a sharp sword with which to strike down the nations. "He will rule them with an iron scepter." He treads the winepress of the fury of the wrath of God Almighty.

~~~~~~

Lord, your anger often makes me uncomfortable. Please teach me that you are rightly angry with wrongdoing that harms your beloved creation.

The Cup of God's Wrath

PSALM 75:6–8

No one from the east or the west
    or from the desert can exalt themselves.
It is God who judges:
    He brings one down, he exalts another.
In the hand of the Lord is a cup
    full of foaming wine mixed with spices;
he pours it out, and all the wicked of the earth
    drink it down to its very dregs.

JEREMIAH 25:15–16

This is what the Lord, the God of Israel, said to me: "Take from my hand this cup filled with the wine of my wrath and make all the nations to whom I send you drink it. When they drink it, they will stagger and go mad because of the sword I will send among them."

REVELATION 16:18–19

Then there came flashes of lightning, rumblings, peals of thunder and a severe earthquake. No earthquake like it has ever occurred since mankind has been on earth, so tremendous was the quake. The great city split into three parts, and the cities of the nations collapsed. God remembered Babylon the Great and gave her the cup filled with the wine of the fury of his wrath.

God will justly make people experience His anger with their sins.

The Justice of God's Wrath

PSALM 7:10–12

My shield is God Most High,
who saves the upright in heart.
God is a righteous judge,
a God who displays his wrath every day.
If he does not relent,
he will sharpen his sword;
he will bend and string his bow.

ISAIAH 13:11–13

I will punish the world for its evil,
the wicked for their sins.
I will put an end to the arrogance of the haughty
and will humble the pride of the ruthless.
I will make people scarcer than pure gold,
more rare than the gold of Ophir.
Therefore I will make the heavens tremble;
and the earth will shake from its place
at the wrath of the LORD Almighty,
in the day of his burning anger.

ROMANS 2:5–6

But because of your stubbornness and your unrepentant heart, you are storing up wrath against yourself for the day of God's wrath, when his righteous judgment will be revealed. God "will repay each person according to what they have done."

~~~

Where is there unrepentance in your life? Confess it to God, and thank Him for being justly angry in places where you are hurting others.

God's Disciplining Wrath

PSALM 76:7–10

> It is you alone who are to be feared.
>> Who can stand before you when you are angry?
> From heaven you pronounced judgment,
>> and the land feared and was quiet—
> when you, God, rose up to judge,
>> to save all the afflicted of the land.
> Surely your wrath against mankind brings you praise,
>> and the survivors of your wrath are restrained.

JOSHUA 22:19–20

But do not rebel against the LORD or against us by building an altar for yourselves, other than the altar of the LORD our God. When Achan son of Zerah was unfaithful in regard to the devoted things, did not wrath come on the whole community of Israel? He was not the only one who died for his sin.

COLOSSIANS 3:4–8

When Christ, who is your life, appears, then you also will appear with him in glory.

Put to death, therefore, whatever belongs to your earthly nature: sexual immorality, impurity, lust, evil desires and greed, which is idolatry. Because of these, the wrath of God is coming. You used to walk in these ways, in the life you once lived. But now you must also rid yourselves of all such things as these.

~~~~~

Lord, your anger corrects me and restrains me from further evil. Your discipline is painful, but thank you that you are putting to death the sins in my life that damage me and my relationships.

God's Wrath and God's Forgiveness

PSALM 85:1–4

You, Lord, showed favor to your land;
　　you restored the fortunes of Jacob.
You forgave the iniquity of your people
　　and covered all their sins.
You set aside all your wrath
　　and turned from your fierce anger.

Restore us again, God our Savior,
　　and put away your displeasure toward us.

EZEKIEL 33:10–11

Son of man, say to the Israelites, "This is what you are saying: 'Our offenses and sins weigh us down, and we are wasting away because of them. How then can we live?'" Say to them, "As surely as I live, declares the Sovereign Lord, I take no pleasure in the death of the wicked, but rather that they turn from their ways and live. Turn! Turn from your evil ways! Why will you die, people of Israel?"

ROMANS 5:7–9

Very rarely will anyone die for a righteous person, though for a good person someone might possibly dare to die. But God demonstrates his own love for us in this: While we were still sinners, Christ died for us. Since we have now been justified by his blood, how much more shall we be saved from God's wrath through him!

～～～

God loves you, forgives you, and restores you. He saved you from His anger by sending Jesus to die for you while you were still a sinner.

God's Avenging Wrath

PSALM 37:7–9

Be still before the LORD
    and wait patiently for him;
do not fret when people succeed in their ways,
    when they carry out their wicked schemes.

Refrain from anger and turn from wrath;
    do not fret—it leads only to evil.
For those who are evil will be destroyed,
    but those who hope in the LORD will inherit the land.

ISAIAH 26:20–21

Go, my people, enter your rooms
    and shut the doors behind you;
hide yourselves for a little while
    until his wrath has passed by.
See, the LORD is coming out of his dwelling
    to punish the people of the earth for their sins.

ROMANS 12:17–19

Do not repay anyone evil for evil. Be careful to do what is right in
the eyes of everyone. If it is possible, as far as it depends on you, live at
peace with everyone. Do not take revenge, my dear friends, but leave
room for God's wrath, for it is written: "It is mine to avenge; I will repay,"
says the Lord.

*When have you been able to commit to God a painful evil that
someone else has done? Tell God how it makes you feel, and ask Him to
bring His justice to the situation.*

Jesus in the Breach of God's Wrath

PSALM 106:21–23

> They forgot the God who saved them,
>   who had done great things in Egypt,
> miracles in the land of Ham
>   and awesome deeds by the Red Sea.
> So he said he would destroy them—
>   had not Moses, his chosen one,
> stood in the breach before him
>   to keep his wrath from destroying them.

EZEKIEL 22:30–31

I looked for someone among them who would build up the wall and stand before me in the gap on behalf of the land so I would not have to destroy it, but I found no one. So I will pour out my wrath on them and consume them with my fiery anger, bringing down on their own heads all they have done, declares the Sovereign LORD.

1 THESSALONIANS 5:9–11

For God did not appoint us to suffer wrath but to receive salvation through our Lord Jesus Christ. He died for us so that, whether we are awake or asleep, we may live together with him. Therefore encourage one another and build each other up, just as in fact you are doing.

~~~~~

Lord, thank you for sending your Son to stand in the breach for humankind and take your fiery anger against sin on His own head. I am so grateful your sacrifice means I get to live together with you.

The God Who Desires Justice

PSALM 101:1–2

> I will sing of your love and justice;
>   to you, LORD, I will sing praise.
> I will be careful to lead a blameless life—
>   when will you come to me?

2 CHRONICLES 19:6–7

He told them, "Consider carefully what you do, because you are not judging for mere mortals but for the LORD, who is with you whenever you give a verdict. Now let the fear of the LORD be on you. Judge carefully, for with the LORD our God there is no injustice or partiality or bribery."

MATTHEW 7:12

So in everything, do to others what you would have them do to you, for this sums up the Law and the Prophets.

～～～

As God is just with you, so He wants you to be just with others.

The God Who Desires Righteousness

PSALM 11:5–7

> The Lord examines the righteous,
>> but the wicked, those who love violence,
>> he hates with a passion.
> On the wicked he will rain
>> fiery coals and burning sulfur;
>> a scorching wind will be their lot.
>
> For the Lord is righteous,
>> he loves justice;
>> the upright will see his face.

HOSEA 10:12

> Sow righteousness for yourselves,
>> reap the fruit of unfailing love,
> and break up your unplowed ground;
>> for it is time to seek the Lord,
> until he comes
>> and showers his righteousness on you.

MATTHEW 6:1–2

Be careful not to practice your righteousness in front of others to be seen by them. If you do, you will have no reward from your Father in heaven.

So when you give to the needy, do not announce it with trumpets, as the hypocrites do in the synagogues and on the streets, to be honored by others. Truly I tell you, they have received their reward in full.

~~~~~

How are you practicing righteousness to gain approval from others? Ask God to teach you what it really looks like to treat others rightly.

Truth

O God of truth, whose living word

upholds whate'er hath breath,

look down on thy creation, Lord,

enslaved by sin and death.

Set up thy standard, Lord, that we
who claim a heav'nly birth,
may march with thee to smite the lies
that vex thy groaning earth.

We fight for truth? We fight for God?
Poor slaves of lies and sin!
They who would fight for thee on earth
must first be pure within.

Then, God of truth, for whom we long,
thou who wilt hear our prayer,
do thine own battle in our hearts,
and slay the falsehood there.

Yea, come: then tried as in the fire,
from ev'ry lie set free,
thy perfect truth shall dwell in us,
and we shall live in thee.

Thomas Hughes, 1859

The Truth of God

PSALM 25:4–5

Show me your ways, Lord,
    teach me your paths.
Guide me in your truth and teach me,
    for you are God my Savior,
    and my hope is in you all day long.

1 SAMUEL 15:27–29

As Samuel turned to leave, Saul caught hold of the hem of his robe, and it tore. Samuel said to him, "The Lord has torn the kingdom of Israel from you today and has given it to one of your neighbors—to one better than you. He who is the Glory of Israel does not lie."

JOHN 14:6–7

Jesus answered, "I am the way and the truth and the life. No one comes to the Father except through me. If you really know me, you will know my Father as well. From now on, you do know him and have seen him."

Lord, you are truth—there is nothing false, untrue, or misleading in you. I want to know your truth.

The God Who Reveals Truth

PSALM 105:16–19

> He called down famine on the land
>> and destroyed all their supplies of food;
> and he sent a man before them—
>> Joseph, sold as a slave.
> They bruised his feet with shackles,
>> his neck was put in irons,
> till what he foretold came to pass,
>> till the word of the LORD proved him true.

ISAIAH 45:19

> I have not spoken in secret,
>> from somewhere in a land of darkness;
> I have not said to Jacob's descendants,
>> 'Seek me in vain.'
> I, the LORD, speak the truth;
>> I declare what is right.

JOHN 18:37–38

"You are a king, then!" said Pilate.

Jesus answered, "You say that I am a king. In fact, the reason I was born and came into the world is to testify to the truth. Everyone on the side of truth listens to me."

"What is truth?" retorted Pilate. With this he went out again to the Jews gathered there and said, "I find no basis for a charge against him."

～～～

God doesn't hide the truth. He testifies to the truth, He speaks truth, and all His words are true.

The Truth of God's Word

PSALM 119:43–44

Never take your word of truth from my mouth,
  for I have put my hope in your laws.
I will always obey your law,
  for ever and ever.

DEUTERONOMY 18:21–22

You may say to yourselves, "How can we know when a message has not been spoken by the LORD?" If what a prophet proclaims in the name of the LORD does not take place or come true, that is a message the LORD has not spoken. That prophet has spoken presumptuously, so do not be alarmed.

2 TIMOTHY 2:14–15

Keep reminding God's people of these things. Warn them before God against quarreling about words; it is of no value, and only ruins those who listen. Do your best to present yourself to God as one approved, a worker who does not need to be ashamed and who correctly handles the word of truth.

~~~~

Where have you been able to keep God's word in your mouth and in your work? Thank Him for the truth of His words—that they lead to truth and accurately describe what is.

The Truth of God's Promises

PSALM 145:13–14

> The LORD is trustworthy in all he promises
> > and faithful in all he does.
> The LORD upholds all who fall
> > and lifts up all who are bowed down.

GENESIS 28:13–15

I am the LORD, the God of your father Abraham and the God of Isaac. I will give you and your descendants the land on which you are lying. . . . All peoples on earth will be blessed through you and your offspring. I am with you and will watch over you wherever you go, and I will bring you back to this land. I will not leave you until I have done what I have promised you.

ROMANS 15:7–9

Accept one another, then, just as Christ accepted you, in order to bring praise to God. For I tell you that Christ has become a servant of the Jews on behalf of God's truth, so that the promises made to the patriarchs might be confirmed and, moreover, that the Gentiles might glorify God for his mercy.

Lord, thank you that all your promises are true. You alone have fulfilled them over thousands of years of faithfulness. Teach me to trust that you are true to me too.

The Truth of God's Spirit

PSALM 119:151

You are near, LORD,
  and all your commands are true.

JOEL 2:28–29

And afterward,
  I will pour out my Spirit on all people.
Your sons and daughters will prophesy,
  your old men will dream dreams,
  your young men will see visions.
Even on my servants, both men and women,
  I will pour out my Spirit in those days.

JOHN 16:13–15

When he, the Spirit of truth, comes, he will guide you into all the truth. He will not speak on his own; he will speak only what he hears, and he will tell you what is yet to come. He will glorify me because it is from me that he will receive what he will make known to you. All that belongs to the Father is mine. That is why I said the Spirit will receive from me what he will make known to you.

~~~~

God poured out His Spirit on you, and the Spirit inside you guides you in all truth.

God's Truth inside His People

PSALM 119:86–88

> All your commands are trustworthy; . . .
>> I have not forsaken your precepts.
> In your unfailing love preserve my life,
>> that I may obey the statutes of your mouth.

ZECHARIAH 8:16–17

"These are the things you are to do: Speak the truth to each other, and render true and sound judgment in your courts; do not plot evil against each other, and do not love to swear falsely. I hate all this," declares the LORD.

2 JOHN 1–3

To the lady chosen by God and to her children, whom I love in the truth—and not I only, but also all who know the truth—because of the truth, which lives in us and will be with us forever:

Grace, mercy and peace from God the Father and from Jesus Christ, the Father's Son, will be with us in truth and love.

When have you spoken falsely or treated another person falsely? Confess this to God, and thank Him for putting His truth in you and with you forever.

The Truth of God's Son

PSALM 9:9–10

> The LORD is a refuge for the oppressed,
>   a stronghold in times of trouble.
> Those who know your name trust in you,
>   for you, LORD, have never forsaken those who seek you.

DEUTERONOMY 18:17–19

The Lord said to me: "What they say is good. I will raise up for them a prophet like you from among their fellow Israelites, and I will put my words in his mouth. He will tell them everything I command him. I myself will call to account anyone who does not listen to my words that the prophet speaks in my name."

1 JOHN 5:20

We know also that the Son of God has come and has given us understanding, so that we may know him who is true. And we are in him who is true by being in his Son Jesus Christ. He is the true God and eternal life.

~~~

Lord, your Son Jesus is truth and eternal life. Thank you for sending Him to reveal that you are true. Turn me from my sins so I can take refuge in Him.

Our Unchanging God

PSALM 125:1–2

> Those who trust in the LORD are like Mount Zion,
>> which cannot be shaken but endures forever.
> As the mountains surround Jerusalem,
>> so the LORD surrounds his people
>> both now and forevermore.

ISAIAH 54:10

> "Though the mountains be shaken
>> and the hills be removed,
> yet my unfailing love for you will not be shaken
>> nor my covenant of peace be removed,"
>> says the LORD, who has compassion on you.

HEBREWS 6:18–20

God did this so that, by two unchangeable things in which it is impossible for God to lie, we who have fled to take hold of the hope set before us may be greatly encouraged. We have this hope as an anchor for the soul, firm and secure. It enters the inner sanctuary behind the curtain, where our forerunner, Jesus, has entered on our behalf. He has become a high priest forever, in the order of Melchizedek.

~~~~~

God's love, faithfulness, and truth never change.

Our Unchanging God in a Changing World

PSALM 102:23–24

> In the course of my life he broke my strength;
> > he cut short my days.
> So I said:
> "Do not take me away, my God, in the midst of my days;
> > your years go on through all generations."

1 SAMUEL 15:29

> [The Lord] is not a human being, that he should change his mind.

1 JOHN 2:15–17

> Do not love the world or anything in the world. If anyone loves the world, love for the Father is not in them. For everything in the world—the lust of the flesh, the lust of the eyes, and the pride of life—comes not from the Father but from the world. The world and its desires pass away, but whoever does the will of God lives forever.

~~~~~~

What word or phrase from the passages above stood out to you? Pause to talk with God about it.

God's Unchanging Law

PSALM 119:97–98

> Oh, how I love your law!
> I meditate on it all day long.
> Your commands are always with me.

JOSHUA 1:8–9

Keep this Book of the Law always on your lips; meditate on it day and night, so that you may be careful to do everything written in it. . . . Have I not commanded you? Be strong and courageous. Do not be afraid; do not be discouraged, for the LORD your God will be with you wherever you go.

MATTHEW 5:17–18

Do not think that I have come to abolish the Law or the Prophets; I have not come to abolish them but to fulfill them. For truly I tell you, until heaven and earth disappear, not the smallest letter, not the least stroke of a pen, will by any means disappear from the Law until everything is accomplished.

~~~

Lord, your commands show me how to live in right relationship with you and with others. Thank you that how to love others well isn't subject to change. Teach me to love as you love.

God's Unchanging Faithfulness

PSALM 117:1–2

Praise the LORD, all you nations;
    extol him, all you peoples.
For great is his love toward us,
    and the faithfulness of the LORD endures forever.

Praise the LORD.

1 KINGS 8:56–57

Praise be to the LORD, who has given rest to his people Israel just as he promised. Not one word has failed of all the good promises he gave through his servant Moses. May the LORD our God be with us as he was with our ancestors; may he never leave us nor forsake us.

1 PETER 4:19

So then, those who suffer according to God's will should commit themselves to their faithful Creator and continue to do good.

Even in times of suffering, God's faithfulness to His character and promises never fails.

God's Unchanging Discipline

PSALM 132:11–12

> The LORD swore an oath to David,
>> a sure oath he will not revoke:
> "One of your own descendants
>> I will place on your throne.
> If your sons keep my covenant
>> and the statutes I teach them,
> then their sons will sit
>> on your throne for ever and ever."

JEREMIAH 44:28–29

"Those who escape the sword and return to the land of Judah from Egypt will be very few. Then the whole remnant of Judah who came to live in Egypt will know whose word will stand—mine or theirs.

"This will be the sign to you that I will punish you in this place," declares the LORD, "so that you will know that my threats of harm against you will surely stand."

HEBREWS 12:5–6

And have you completely forgotten this word of encouragement that addresses you as a father addresses his son? It says,

> "My son, do not make light of the Lord's discipline,
>> and do not lose heart when he rebukes you,
> because the Lord disciplines the one he loves,
>> and he chastens everyone he accepts as his son."

~~~~~~~~

When have you taken God's discipline as a sign of displeasure?
Talk with Him about it, asking Him to show you how His consistent
discipline is a sign of His true relationship with you.

God's Unchanging Forgiveness

PSALM 62:1–2

Truly my soul finds rest in God;
    my salvation comes from him.
Truly he is my rock and my salvation;
    he is my fortress, I will never be shaken.

JONAH 3:8–10

"Let everyone call urgently on God. Let them give up their evil ways and their violence. Who knows? God may yet relent and with compassion turn from his fierce anger so that we will not perish."

When God saw what they did and how they turned from their evil ways, he relented and did not bring on them the destruction he had threatened.

ACTS 3:17–21

Now, fellow Israelites, I know that you acted in ignorance, as did your leaders. But this is how God fulfilled what he had foretold through all the prophets, saying that his Messiah would suffer. Repent, then, and turn to God, so that your sins may be wiped out, that times of refreshing may come from the Lord, and that he may send the Messiah, who has been appointed for you—even Jesus. Heaven must receive him until the time comes for God to restore everything, as he promised long ago through his holy prophets.

~~~~~~~~

Lord, I feel ashamed of my sin and the harm I've caused in my pride. Please remind me that your forgiveness is sure when I repent and turn to you.

God Unchanging Forever

PSALM 102:12

But you, LORD, sit enthroned forever;
your renown endures through all generations.

ECCLESIASTES 3:14–15

I know that everything God does will endure forever; nothing can be added to it and nothing taken from it. God does it so that people will fear him.

Whatever is has already been,
and what will be has been before;
and God will call the past to account.

HEBREWS 1:10–12

He also says,

"In the beginning, Lord, you laid the foundations of the earth,
and the heavens are the work of your hands.
They will perish, but you remain;
they will all wear out like a garment.
You will roll them up like a robe;
like a garment they will be changed.
But you remain the same,
and your years will never end."

~~~~~

God remains the same—yesterday, today, and forever.

The Lord Our God Is One

PSALM 89:16–18

They rejoice in your name all day long;
  they celebrate your righteousness.
For you are their glory and strength,
  and by your favor you exalt our horn.
Indeed, our shield belongs to the LORD,
  our king to the Holy One of Israel.

DEUTERONOMY 6:4–5

Hear, O Israel: The LORD our God, the LORD is one. Love the LORD your God with all your heart and with all your soul and with all your strength.

MARK 12:28–31

One of the teachers of the law came and heard them debating. Noticing that Jesus had given them a good answer, he asked him, "Of all the commandments, which is the most important?"

"The most important one," answered Jesus, "is this: 'Hear, O Israel: The Lord our God, the Lord is one. Love the Lord your God with all your heart and with all your soul and with all your mind and with all your strength.' The second is this: 'Love your neighbor as yourself.' There is no commandment greater than these."

~~~~~~

What does the truth that God is one and not many mean to you? Share your thoughts and praise with Him.

The One God over All "Gods"

PSALM 68:7–8

> When you, God, went out before your people,
>   when you marched through the wilderness,
> the earth shook, the heavens poured down rain,
>   before God, the One of Sinai,
>   before God, the God of Israel.

EXODUS 20:1–3

And God spoke all these words:

"I am the LORD your God, who brought you out of Egypt, out of the land of slavery.

"You shall have no other gods before me."

1 CORINTHIANS 8:3–4

Whoever loves God is known by God.

So then, about eating food sacrificed to idols: We know that "An idol is nothing at all in the world" and that "There is no God but one."

~~~~~

Lord, thank you that you are the one true God. I don't have to try to appease other gods or divide my loyalty. Teach me to worship you and you alone.

The One God of All the Earth

PSALM 76:11–12

Make vows to the LORD your God and fulfill them;
> let all the neighboring lands
> bring gifts to the One to be feared.
He breaks the spirit of rulers;
> he is feared by the kings of the earth.

1 KINGS 8:59–60

And may these words of mine, which I have prayed before the LORD, be near to the LORD our God day and night, that he may uphold the cause of his servant and the cause of his people Israel according to each day's need, so that all the peoples of the earth may know that the LORD is God and that there is no other.

ROMANS 3:29–30

Or is God the God of Jews only? Is he not the God of Gentiles too? Yes, of Gentiles too, since there is only one God, who will justify the circumcised by faith and the uncircumcised through that same faith.

God is the one God of all the nations of the earth, and He reveals himself to them through His relationship with His people.

The One God Who Is Three in One

PSALM 71:22–23

> I will praise you with the harp
>> for your faithfulness, my God;
> I will sing praise to you with the lyre,
>> Holy One of Israel.
> My lips will shout for joy
>> when I sing praise to you.

GENESIS 3:21–22

The Lord God made garments of skin for Adam and his wife and clothed them. And the Lord God said, "The man has now become like one of us, knowing good and evil."

ACTS 2:32–33

God has raised this Jesus to life, and we are all witnesses of it. Exalted to the right hand of God, he has received from the Father the promised Holy Spirit and has poured out what you now see and hear.

~~~~~

Where in your life do you tend to reduce God to one dimension when He is really three in one? Ask God for understanding, to more fully grasp who He is.

The One God Unlike All Others

PSALM 3:3–4

But you, LORD, are a shield around me,
    my glory, the One who lifts my head high.
I call out to the LORD,
    and he answers me from his holy mountain.

1 KINGS 18:37–39

"Answer me, LORD, answer me, so these people will know that you, LORD, are God, and that you are turning their hearts back again."

Then the fire of the LORD fell and burned up the sacrifice, the wood, the stones and the soil, and also licked up the water in the trench.

When all the people saw this, they fell prostrate and cried, "The LORD—he is God! The LORD—he is God!"

JAMES 2:19

You believe that there is one God. Good! Even the demons believe that—and shudder.

~~~~~~

Lord, too often I assume you have the flaws, weaknesses, and blind spots of the people around me. Thank you for being the one unlike everyone else—glorious, good, and all-powerful.

The One God Who Draws Near

PSALM 132:2–5

> He swore an oath to the Lord,
>   he made a vow to the Mighty One of Jacob:
> "I will not enter my house
>   or go to my bed,
> I will allow no sleep to my eyes
>   or slumber to my eyelids,
> till I find a place for the Lord,
>   a dwelling for the Mighty One of Jacob."

ISAIAH 37:14–17

Hezekiah received the letter from the messengers and read it. Then he went up to the temple of the Lord and spread it out before the Lord. And Hezekiah prayed to the Lord: "Lord Almighty, the God of Israel, enthroned between the cherubim, you alone are God over all the kingdoms of the earth. You have made heaven and earth. Give ear, Lord, and hear; open your eyes, Lord, and see."

JOHN 14:9–10

Anyone who has seen me has seen the Father. How can you say, "Show us the Father"? Don't you believe that I am in the Father, and that the Father is in me? The words I say to you I do not speak on my own authority. Rather, it is the Father, living in me, who is doing his work.

～～～

In His presence, care, and incarnation, the one true God draws near His people.

The One Savior for All People

PSALM 78:40–42

> How often they rebelled against him in the wilderness
> and grieved him in the wasteland!
> Again and again they put God to the test;
> they vexed the Holy One of Israel.
> They did not remember his power—
> the day he redeemed them from the oppressor.

HOSEA 13:4–5

> But I have been the LORD your God
> ever since you came out of Egypt.
> You shall acknowledge no God but me,
> no Savior except me.
> I cared for you in the wilderness,
> in the land of burning heat.

1 TIMOTHY 2:3–6

This is good, and pleases God our Savior, who wants all people to be saved and to come to a knowledge of the truth. For there is one God and one mediator between God and mankind, the man Christ Jesus, who gave himself as a ransom for all people. This has now been witnessed to at the proper time.

~~~

How has sharing salvation in Jesus Christ bound you together with other believers? Thank God for providing the same savior for all people, and for bringing you to a knowledge of the truth.

God Is Ultimate Reality

PSALM 14:1

The fool says in his heart,
"There is no God."

EZEKIEL 1:26–28

Above the vault over their heads was what looked like a throne of lapis lazuli, and high above on the throne was a figure like that of a man. I saw that from what appeared to be his waist up he looked like glowing metal, as if full of fire, and that from there down he looked like fire; and brilliant light surrounded him. Like the appearance of a rainbow in the clouds on a rainy day, so was the radiance around him.

This was the appearance of the likeness of the glory of the LORD. When I saw it, I fell facedown.

COLOSSIANS 2:15–17

Having disarmed the powers and authorities, [Jesus] made a public spectacle of them, triumphing over them by the cross.

Therefore do not let anyone judge you by what you eat or drink, or with regard to a religious festival, a New Moon celebration or a Sabbath day. These are a shadow of the things that were to come; the reality, however, is found in Christ.

～～～

Lord, you are true reality, the person who brings meaning to all of life. I want to see you as you are, even when you're beyond my senses and understanding.

The God of Reality Seen and Unseen

PSALM 89:6–7

Who in the skies above can compare with the LORD?
    Who is like the LORD among the heavenly beings?
In the council of the holy ones God is greatly feared;
    he is more awesome than all who surround him.

2 KINGS 6:16–17

"Don't be afraid," the prophet answered. "Those who are with us are more than those who are with them."

And Elisha prayed, "Open his eyes, LORD, so that he may see." Then the LORD opened the servant's eyes, and he looked and saw the hills full of horses and chariots of fire all around Elisha.

LUKE 9:28–30, 34–35

[Jesus] took Peter, John and James with him and went up onto a mountain to pray. As he was praying, the appearance of his face changed, and his clothes became as bright as a flash of lightning. Two men, Moses and Elijah, appeared in glorious splendor, talking with Jesus. . . .

A cloud appeared and covered them, and they were afraid as they entered the cloud. A voice came from the cloud, saying, "This is my Son, whom I have chosen; listen to him."

~~~~

God commands all of reality—both the realm you can see and the realm you can't see.

God, the Reality of Life

PSALM 27:1

The Lord is my light and my salvation—
whom shall I fear?
The Lord is the stronghold of my life—
of whom shall I be afraid?

ISAIAH 42:5

This is what God the Lord says—
the Creator of the heavens, who stretches them out,
who spreads out the earth with all that springs from it,
who gives breath to its people,
and life to those who walk on it.

JOHN 12:23–26

Jesus replied, "The hour has come for the Son of Man to be glorified. Very truly I tell you, unless a kernel of wheat falls to the ground and dies, it remains only a single seed. But if it dies, it produces many seeds. Anyone who loves their life will lose it, while anyone who hates their life in this world will keep it for eternal life. Whoever serves me must follow me; and where I am, my servant also will be.

When have you looked to something other than God for life?
Talk with Him about it, thanking Him that He gives life and is life.

God, the Reality of Wisdom

PSALM 36:1–3

I have a message from God in my heart
　　concerning the sinfulness of the wicked:
There is no fear of God
　　before their eyes.

In their own eyes they flatter themselves
　　too much to detect or hate their sin.
The words of their mouths are wicked and deceitful;
　　they fail to act wisely or do good.

PROVERBS 8:12–14

I, wisdom, dwell together with prudence;
　　I possess knowledge and discretion.
To fear the LORD is to hate evil;
　　I hate pride and arrogance,
　　evil behavior and perverse speech.
Counsel and sound judgment are mine;
　　I have insight, I have power.

1 CORINTHIANS 1:18–19

For the message of the cross is foolishness to those who are perishing, but to us who are being saved it is the power of God. For it is written:

"I will destroy the wisdom of the wise;
　　the intelligence of the intelligent I will frustrate."

~~~

Lord, thank you that you are true wisdom. When pride and arrogance blind me to my sin, please turn me back to you and teach me your ways.

God, the Reality of Strength

PSALM 103:15–16

> The life of mortals is like grass,
>> they flourish like a flower of the field;
> the wind blows over it and it is gone,
>> and its place remembers it no more.

ISAIAH 40:29–31

> He gives strength to the weary
>> and increases the power of the weak.
> Even youths grow tired and weary,
>> and young men stumble and fall;
> but those who hope in the LORD
>> will renew their strength.
> They will soar on wings like eagles;
>> they will run and not grow weary,
>> they will walk and not be faint.

REVELATION 11:16–17

> And the twenty-four elders, who were seated on their thrones before God, fell on their faces and worshiped God, saying:

> "We give thanks to you, Lord God Almighty,
>> the One who is and who was,
> because you have taken your great power
>> and have begun to reign."

～～～

Human strength wanes over time, but the true strength of God always was and always will be.

God, the Reality of Authority

PSALM 89:11–13

> The heavens are yours, and yours also the earth;
>> you founded the world and all that is in it.
> You created the north and the south;
>> Tabor and Hermon sing for joy at your name.
> Your arm is endowed with power;
>> your hand is strong, your right hand exalted.

ZECHARIAH 14:9

The LORD will be king over the whole earth. On that day there will be one LORD, and his name the only name.

1 CORINTHIANS 15:20–24

But Christ has indeed been raised from the dead, the firstfruits of those who have fallen asleep. For since death came through a man, the resurrection of the dead comes also through a man. For as in Adam all die, so in Christ all will be made alive. But each in turn: Christ, the firstfruits; then, when he comes, those who belong to him. Then the end will come, when he hands over the kingdom to God the Father after he has destroyed all dominion, authority and power.

~~~~~

Where have you seen God's true authority reigning even in a place under temporary human authority? Pray and thank Him that He is the eternal King who is bringing His rule over all creation.

God, the Reality of Unity

PSALM 133:1–3

How good and pleasant it is
    when God's people live together in unity!

It is like precious oil poured on the head,
    running down on the beard,
running down on Aaron's beard,
    down on the collar of his robe.
It is as if the dew of Hermon
    were falling on Mount Zion.
For there the LORD bestows his blessing,
    even life forevermore.

2 CHRONICLES 30:12

Also in Judah the hand of God was on the people to give them unity of mind to carry out what the king and his officials had ordered, following the word of the LORD.

JOHN 17:22–23

I have given them the glory that you gave me, that they may be one as we are one—I in them and you in me—so that they may be brought to complete unity. Then the world will know that you sent me and have loved them even as you have loved me.

Lord, the world is full of division and strife. Thank you for bringing love and unity through your Spirit. Please teach your people to be one as you are one.

God's Truth Sets Us Free

PSALM 119:45–47

I will walk about in freedom,
> for I have sought out your precepts.
I will speak of your statutes before kings
> and will not be put to shame,
for I delight in your commands
> because I love them.

ISAIAH 49:8–9

This is what the LORD says:

"In the time of my favor I will answer you,
> and in the day of salvation I will help you;
I will keep you and will make you
> to be a covenant for the people,
to restore the land
> and to reassign its desolate inheritances,
to say to the captives, 'Come out,'
> and to those in darkness, 'Be free!'"

JOHN 8:31–32

To the Jews who had believed him, Jesus said, "If you hold to my teaching, you are really my disciples. Then you will know the truth, and the truth will set you free."

True freedom is found in the commands, promises, and salvation of Jesus.

God's Unchanging Covenant

PSALM 46:1–3

God is our refuge and strength,
an ever-present help in trouble.
Therefore we will not fear, though the earth give way
and the mountains fall into the heart of the sea,
though its waters roar and foam
and the mountains quake with their surging.

GENESIS 17:5–7

No longer will you be called Abram; your name will be Abraham, for I have made you a father of many nations. I will make you very fruitful; I will make nations of you, and kings will come from you. I will establish my covenant as an everlasting covenant between me and you and your descendants after you for the generations to come, to be your God and the God of your descendants after you.

HEBREWS 7:20–22

Others became priests without any oath, but [Jesus] became a priest with an oath when God said to him:

"The Lord has sworn
and will not change his mind:
'You are a priest forever.'"

Because of this oath, Jesus has become the guarantor of a better covenant.

~~~~~~

Which of God's promises do you struggle to believe? Ask Him to hold your doubts and remind you of His faithfulness in the past.

God Delights in Truth

PSALM 15:1–3

> Lord, who may dwell in your sacred tent?
>> Who may live on your holy mountain?
>
> The one whose walk is blameless,
>> who does what is righteous,
>> who speaks the truth from their heart;
> whose tongue utters no slander,
>> who does no wrong to a neighbor,
>> and casts no slur on others.

PROVERBS 12:22

> The Lord detests lying lips,
>> but he delights in people who are trustworthy.

3 JOHN 3–4

It gave me great joy when some believers came and testified about your faithfulness to the truth, telling how you continue to walk in it. I have no greater joy than to hear that my children are walking in the truth.

~~~~

Lord, thank you for being the truth, and for delighting in truth. Please keep my mouth from half-truths and my mind from unreal assumptions. I want to walk in your truth.

Good

Jesus has been so good to me,

no other friend so kind could be;

safely keeps me every day

free from sin and in the way;

ne'er can I such love repay,

He's so good to me.

Jesus has been so good to me,

none so fair, so dear as He:

hallelujah! He is mine,

keeping me by grace divine,

and His glories in me shine,

He's so good to me.

Jesus is good to me,

Jesus is good to me;

safely keeps me from the wrong,

in the conflict makes me strong,

blesses all my journey long,

He's so good to me.

Daniel Otis Teasley, 1911

God Is Good

PSALM 106:1–2

> Give thanks to the LORD, for he is good;
>   his love endures forever.
>
> Who can proclaim the mighty acts of the LORD
>   or fully declare his praise?

JEREMIAH 32:40–41

I will make an everlasting covenant with them: I will never stop doing good to them, and I will inspire them to fear me, so that they will never turn away from me. I will rejoice in doing them good and will assuredly plant them in this land with all my heart and soul.

1 JOHN 1:5–7

This is the message we have heard from him and declare to you: God is light; in him there is no darkness at all. If we claim to have fellowship with him and yet walk in the darkness, we lie and do not live out the truth. But if we walk in the light, as he is in the light, we have fellowship with one another, and the blood of Jesus, his Son, purifies us from all sin.

~~~

God is good, and there is no evil in Him. He will never stop doing good to you.

No One Good
Except God Alone

PSALM 53:1

The fool says in his heart,
"There is no God."
They are corrupt, and their ways are vile;
there is no one who does good.

JUDGES 17:5–6

Now this man Micah had a shrine, and he made an ephod and some household gods and installed one of his sons as his priest. In those days Israel had no king; everyone did as they saw fit.

MARK 10:17–18

As Jesus started on his way, a man ran up to him and fell on his knees before him. "Good teacher," he asked, "what must I do to inherit eternal life?"

"Why do you call me good?" Jesus answered. "No one is good—except God alone."

~~~~~~

When have you seen God's goodness stand out amid human self-centeredness? Thank Him for being who He is, and ask Him to guide you in His will and not your own.

God Is Good to the Good and the Wicked

PSALM 145:9

> The Lord is good to all;
>> he has compassion on all he has made.

JEREMIAH 12:1–2

> You are always righteous, Lord,
>> when I bring a case before you.
> Yet I would speak with you about your justice:
>> Why does the way of the wicked prosper?
>> Why do all the faithless live at ease?
> You have planted them, and they have taken root;
>> they grow and bear fruit.
> You are always on their lips
>> but far from their hearts.

MATTHEW 5:43–45

You have heard that it was said, "Love your neighbor and hate your enemy." But I tell you, love your enemies and pray for those who persecute you, that you may be children of your Father in heaven. He causes his sun to rise on the evil and the good, and sends rain on the righteous and the unrighteous.

~~~~~~

Lord, sometimes I feel cheated that you are good to those who aren't good to you. I don't want to feel this envy. Thank you for being good to those who don't deserve it, because that's me too.

God's Good Discipline

PSALM 119:65–68

Do good to your servant
according to your word, Lord.
Teach me knowledge and good judgment,
for I trust your commands.
Before I was afflicted I went astray,
but now I obey your word.
You are good, and what you do is good;
teach me your decrees.

JOSHUA 23:14–15

You know with all your heart and soul that not one of all the good promises the Lord your God gave you has failed. Every promise has been fulfilled; not one has failed. But just as all the good things the Lord your God has promised you have come to you, so he will bring on you all the evil things he has threatened, until the Lord your God has destroyed you from this good land he has given you.

HEBREWS 12:10–11

They disciplined us for a little while as they thought best; but God disciplines us for our good, in order that we may share in his holiness. No discipline seems pleasant at the time, but painful. Later on, however, it produces a harvest of righteousness and peace for those who have been trained by it.

~~~~~~

God's discipline is painful, but it is a good tool for cultivating holiness, righteousness, and peace.

God's Eternal Goodness

PSALM 118:28–29

> You are my God, and I will praise you;
> you are my God, and I will exalt you.
>
> Give thanks to the LORD, for he is good;
> his love endures forever.

1 CHRONICLES 16:34–36

> Give thanks to the LORD, for he is good;
> his love endures forever.
> Cry out, "Save us, God our Savior;
> gather us and deliver us from the nations,
> that we may give thanks to your holy name,
> and glory in your praise."
> Praise be to the LORD, the God of Israel,
> from everlasting to everlasting.

HEBREWS 9:11–12

But when Christ came as high priest of the good things that are now already here, he went through the greater and more perfect tabernacle that is not made with human hands, that is to say, is not a part of this creation. He did not enter by means of the blood of goats and calves; but he entered the Most Holy Place once for all by his own blood, thus obtaining eternal redemption.

~~~~~~

What future event or circumstance makes you feel anxious? Talk with God about it. Thank Him that His goodness endures forever—it will never run out.

God's Goodness Reflected in His People

PSALM 1:1–3

> Blessed is the one
> who does not walk in step with the wicked
> or stand in the way that sinners take
> or sit in the company of mockers,
> but whose delight is in the law of the LORD,
> and who meditates on his law day and night.
> That person is like a tree planted by streams of water,
> which yields its fruit in season.

AMOS 5:14–15

> Seek good, not evil,
> that you may live.
> Then the LORD God Almighty will be with you,
> just as you say he is.
> Hate evil, love good;
> maintain justice in the courts.
> Perhaps the LORD God Almighty will have mercy
> on the remnant of Joseph.

PHILEMON 6–7

I pray that your partnership with us in the faith may be effective in deepening your understanding of every good thing we share for the sake of Christ. Your love has given me great joy and encouragement, because you, brother, have refreshed the hearts of the Lord's people.

~~~~~

Lord, you are good, full of wisdom and love and justice. Through the tending of your Spirit, please make me more and more like you. Plant me by streams of your living water.

The Goodness of God's Rescue

PSALM 107:1–3

Give thanks to the LORD, for he is good;
  his love endures forever.

Let the redeemed of the LORD tell their story—
  those he redeemed from the hand of the foe,
those he gathered from the lands,
  from east and west, from north and south.

JEREMIAH 29:10–12

This is what the LORD says: "When seventy years are completed
for Babylon, I will come to you and fulfill my good promise to bring
you back to this place. For I know the plans I have for you," declares the
LORD, "plans to prosper you and not to harm you, plans to give you hope
and a future. Then you will call on me and come and pray to me, and I
will listen to you."

JOHN 10:9–11

I am the gate; whoever enters through me will be saved. They will
come in and go out, and find pasture. The thief comes only to steal and kill
and destroy; I have come that they may have life, and have it to the full.
  I am the good shepherd. The good shepherd lays down his life for
the sheep.

~~~~~

*God's goodness redeems His people through self-giving sacrifice,
freeing them from sin and exile and bringing them into His
abundant life.*

God Is Perfect

PSALM 18:30–31

As for God, his way is perfect:
The Lord's word is flawless;
he shields all who take refuge in him.
For who is God besides the Lord?
And who is the Rock except our God?

DEUTERONOMY 32:3–4

I will proclaim the name of the Lord.
Oh, praise the greatness of our God!
He is the Rock, his works are perfect,
and all his ways are just.
A faithful God who does no wrong,
upright and just is he.

MATTHEW 5:46–48

If you love those who love you, what reward will you get? Are not even the tax collectors doing that? And if you greet only your own people, what are you doing more than others? Do not even pagans do that? Be perfect, therefore, as your heavenly Father is perfect.

What word or phrase from the passages above stood out to you? Pause to talk with God about it.

God Does No Wrong

PSALM 92:12–15

The righteous will flourish like a palm tree,
　　they will grow like a cedar of Lebanon;
planted in the house of the LORD,
　　they will flourish in the courts of our God.
They will still bear fruit in old age,
　　they will stay fresh and green,
proclaiming, "The LORD is upright;
　　he is my Rock, and there is no wickedness in him."

JOB 34:10–12

So listen to me, you men of understanding.
　　Far be it from God to do evil,
　　from the Almighty to do wrong.
He repays everyone for what they have done;
　　he brings on them what their conduct deserves.
It is unthinkable that God would do wrong,
　　that the Almighty would pervert justice.

1 JOHN 3:6–7

No one who lives in [Christ] keeps on sinning. No one who continues to sin has either seen him or known him.

Dear children, do not let anyone lead you astray. The one who does what is right is righteous, just as he is righteous.

～～～

Lord, thank you for never doing wrong. I confess I sometimes feel like you've wronged me or others. Please show me how you never sin in any of your relationships with all your creation.

God's Perfect Law

PSALM 119:94–96

Save me, for I am yours;
> I have sought out your precepts.
The wicked are waiting to destroy me,
> but I will ponder your statutes.
To all perfection I see a limit,
> but your commands are boundless.

2 SAMUEL 22:31

As for God, his way is perfect:
> The Lord's word is flawless;
> he shields all who take refuge in him.

JAMES 1:23–25

Anyone who listens to the word but does not do what it says is like someone who looks at his face in a mirror and, after looking at himself, goes away and immediately forgets what he looks like. But whoever looks intently into the perfect law that gives freedom, and continues in it—not forgetting what they have heard, but doing it—they will be blessed in what they do.

~~~

God's commands are perfect: they wholly and completely reveal right relationships and freedom.

The Perfect God
of Imperfect People

PSALM 18:25–27

To the faithful you show yourself faithful,
    to the blameless you show yourself blameless,
to the pure you show yourself pure,
    but to the devious you show yourself shrewd.
You save the humble
    but bring low those whose eyes are haughty.

EZEKIEL 18:28–29

Because they consider all the offenses they have committed and turn away from them, that person will surely live; they will not die. Yet the Israelites say, "The way of the Lord is not just." Are my ways unjust, people of Israel? Is it not your ways that are unjust?

2 CORINTHIANS 12:8–9

Three times I pleaded with the Lord to take it away from me. But he said to me, "My grace is sufficient for you, for my power is made perfect in weakness." Therefore I will boast all the more gladly about my weaknesses, so that Christ's power may rest on me.

In what area of your life are you keenly aware of your imperfections? Share what you're feeling with God, thanking Him that He is perfect even amid your weaknesses.

God's Perfect Holiness

PSALM 119:1–3

> Blessed are those whose ways are blameless,
> who walk according to the law of the LORD.
> Blessed are those who keep his statutes
> and seek him with all their heart—
> they do no wrong
> but follow his ways.

LEVITICUS 19:1–2

The LORD said to Moses, "Speak to the entire assembly of Israel and say to them: 'Be holy because I, the LORD your God, am holy.'"

1 PETER 1:14–16

As obedient children, do not conform to the evil desires you had when you lived in ignorance. But just as he who called you is holy, so be holy in all you do; for it is written: "Be holy, because I am holy."

Lord, you are perfectly holy: you are wholly other, and you are other because you are wholly good and loving. Thank you that you want me to be like you, conforming me to the perfect image of your Son.

God's Perfect Justice

PSALM 19:9–10

The fear of the LORD is pure,
enduring forever.
The decrees of the LORD are firm,
and all of them are righteous.

They are more precious than gold,
than much pure gold;
they are sweeter than honey,
than honey from the honeycomb.

GENESIS 18:24–25

What if there are fifty righteous people in the city? Will you really sweep it away and not spare the place for the sake of the fifty righteous people in it? Far be it from you to do such a thing—to kill the righteous with the wicked, treating the righteous and the wicked alike. Far be it from you! Will not the Judge of all the earth do right?

MATTHEW 19:18–21

Jesus replied, "'You shall not murder, you shall not commit adultery, you shall not steal, you shall not give false testimony, honor your father and mother,' and 'love your neighbor as yourself.'"

"All these I have kept," the young man said. "What do I still lack?"

Jesus answered, "If you want to be perfect, go, sell your possessions and give to the poor, and you will have treasure in heaven. Then come, follow me."

~~~

God is the judge of all the earth, and His justice is equitable, truthful, loving, and righteous to all.

The Perfect God
Makes His People Perfect

PSALM 40:5

Many, Lord my God,
>   are the wonders you have done,
>   the things you planned for us.
None can compare with you;
>   were I to speak and tell of your deeds,
>   they would be too many to declare.

ISAIAH 25:1

Lord, you are my God;
>   I will exalt you and praise your name,
for in perfect faithfulness
>   you have done wonderful things,
>   things planned long ago.

EPHESIANS 5:25–27

Christ loved the church and gave himself up for her to make her holy, cleansing her by the washing with water through the word, and to present her to himself as a radiant church, without stain or wrinkle or any other blemish, but holy and blameless.

~~~~

How has God been making you more perfect recently? Thank Him for loving you, giving himself up for you, and making you holy and blameless—as He has always planned to do.

God Is Gracious

PSALM 67:1–2

> May God be gracious to us and bless us
> and make his face shine on us—
> so that your ways may be known on earth,
> your salvation among all nations.

ISAIAH 33:2–3

> Lord, be gracious to us;
> we long for you.
> Be our strength every morning,
> our salvation in time of distress.
> At the uproar of your army, the peoples flee;
> when you rise up, the nations scatter.

JOHN 1:16–18

Out of his fullness we have all received grace in place of grace already given. For the law was given through Moses; grace and truth came through Jesus Christ. No one has ever seen God, but the one and only Son, who is himself God and is in closest relationship with the Father, has made him known.

~~~~~

Lord, thank you for lavishing your grace on me, giving me your strength, truth, and salvation. Please use your grace in my life to show yourself to those around me.

Our Gracious God with Us

PSALM 5:1–3

> Listen to my words, LORD,
>> consider my lament.
> Hear my cry for help,
>> my King and my God,
>> for to you I pray.
>
> In the morning, LORD, you hear my voice;
>> in the morning I lay my requests before you
>> and wait expectantly.

2 KINGS 13:23

But the LORD was gracious to them and had compassion and showed concern for them because of his covenant with Abraham, Isaac and Jacob. To this day he has been unwilling to destroy them or banish them from his presence.

HEBREWS 2:16–17

For surely it is not angels [Jesus] helps, but Abraham's descendants. For this reason he had to be made like them, fully human in every way, in order that he might become a merciful and faithful high priest in service to God, and that he might make atonement for the sins of the people.

~~~~~~

It is a good gift from God that He hears you, sees you, and is with you.

God's Gracious Promises

PSALM 119:57–58

You are my portion, LORD;
  I have promised to obey your words.
I have sought your face with all my heart;
  be gracious to me according to your promise.

GENESIS 21:1–2

Now the LORD was gracious to Sarah as he had said, and the LORD did for Sarah what he had promised. Sarah became pregnant and bore a son to Abraham in his old age, at the very time God had promised him.

ROMANS 4:16–17

Therefore, the promise comes by faith, so that it may be by grace and may be guaranteed to all Abraham's offspring—not only to those who are of the law but also to those who have the faith of Abraham. He is the father of us all. As it is written: "I have made you a father of many nations." He is our father in the sight of God, in whom he believed—the God who gives life to the dead and calls into being things that were not.

Where do you feel like God has not fulfilled His promises to you? Talk with Him about it, asking Him to remind you of the grace He has shown in the past—and will continue to show to His people.

God's Gracious Provision

PSALM 78:14–16

He guided them with the cloud by day
    and with light from the fire all night.
He split the rocks in the wilderness
    and gave them water as abundant as the seas;
he brought streams out of a rocky crag
    and made water flow down like rivers.

EZRA 9:8–9

But now, for a brief moment, the LORD our God has been gracious in leaving us a remnant and giving us a firm place in his sanctuary, and so our God gives light to our eyes and a little relief in our bondage. . . . He has granted us new life to rebuild the house of our God and repair its ruins, and he has given us a wall of protection in Judah and Jerusalem.

ACTS 4:33–35

With great power the apostles continued to testify to the resurrection of the Lord Jesus. And God's grace was so powerfully at work in them all that there were no needy persons among them. For from time to time those who owned land or houses sold them, brought the money from the sales and put it at the apostles' feet, and it was distributed to anyone who had need.

~~~~~

Lord, you guide me, sustain me, protect me, and provide for me.
All these things are gifts from your hand. Thank you.

God's Grace Even When We're Not Gracious

PSALM 143:1–2

> LORD, hear my prayer,
>> listen to my cry for mercy;
> in your faithfulness and righteousness
>> come to my relief.
> Do not bring your servant into judgment,
>> for no one living is righteous before you.

ISAIAH 26:9–10

> When your judgments come upon the earth,
>> the people of the world learn righteousness.
> But when grace is shown to the wicked,
>> they do not learn righteousness;
> even in a land of uprightness they go on doing evil
>> and do not regard the majesty of the LORD.

MARK 3:2, 4–5

Some of them were looking for a reason to accuse Jesus, so they watched him closely to see if he would heal him on the Sabbath. . . .

Then Jesus asked them, "Which is lawful on the Sabbath: to do good or to do evil, to save life or to kill?" But they remained silent.

He looked around at them in anger and, deeply distressed at their stubborn hearts, said to the man, "Stretch out your hand." He stretched it out, and his hand was completely restored.

~~~~~~

Even when you are faithless, stubborn, or stingy, God is gracious to you.

God's Gracious Forgiveness

PSALM 25:16–18

Turn to me and be gracious to me,
for I am lonely and afflicted.
Relieve the troubles of my heart
and free me from my anguish.
Look on my affliction and my distress
and take away all my sins.

HOSEA 14:1–2

Return, Israel, to the LORD your God.
Your sins have been your downfall!
Take words with you
and return to the LORD.
Say to him:
"Forgive all our sins
and receive us graciously,
that we may offer the fruit of our lips."

ROMANS 5:20–21

The law was brought in so that the trespass might increase. But where sin increased, grace increased all the more, so that, just as sin reigned in death, so also grace might reign through righteousness to bring eternal life through Jesus Christ our Lord.

When have you known God's gracious forgiveness in your life? Praise Him that wherever your sin increases, His grace increases all the more.

God's Gracious Salvation

PSALM 116:1–4

> I love the LORD, for he heard my voice;
> > he heard my cry for mercy.
> Because he turned his ear to me,
> > I will call on him as long as I live.
>
> The cords of death entangled me,
> > the anguish of the grave came over me;
> > I was overcome by distress and sorrow.
> Then I called on the name of the LORD:
> > "LORD, save me!"

ISAIAH 30:19

People of Zion, who live in Jerusalem, you will weep no more. How gracious he will be when you cry for help! As soon as he hears, he will answer you.

ROMANS 5:15, 17

But the gift is not like the trespass. For if the many died by the trespass of the one man, how much more did God's grace and the gift that came by the grace of the one man, Jesus Christ, overflow to the many! . . . For if, by the trespass of the one man, death reigned through that one man, how much more will those who receive God's abundant provision of grace and of the gift of righteousness reign in life through the one man, Jesus Christ!

~~~

Lord, thank you for your grace that overcomes sin and death through the gift of your Son Jesus. You are so gracious to hear me when I cry out to you.

God Is Humble

PSALM 113:5–6

Who is like the LORD our God,
the One who sits enthroned on high,
who stoops down to look
on the heavens and the earth?

HOSEA 11:4

I led them with cords of human kindness,
with ties of love.
To them I was like one who lifts
a little child to the cheek,
and I bent down to feed them.

PHILIPPIANS 2:5–8

In your relationships with one another, have the same mindset as
Christ Jesus:

Who, being in very nature God,
did not consider equality with God something to be used
to his own advantage;
rather, he made himself nothing
by taking the very nature of a servant,
being made in human likeness.
And being found in appearance as a man,
he humbled himself
by becoming obedient to death—
even death on a cross!

~~~~~

*God is glorious and all-powerful—yet humbly pursues a loving,
self-giving relationship with you.*

The Humility of God's Incarnation

PSALM 22:9–11

Yet you brought me out of the womb;
> you made me trust in you, even at my mother's breast.

From birth I was cast on you;
> from my mother's womb you have been my God.

Do not be far from me,
> for trouble is near
> and there is no one to help.

ISAIAH 7:14

Therefore the Lord himself will give you a sign: The virgin will conceive and give birth to a son, and will call him Immanuel.

GALATIANS 4:4–5

But when the set time had fully come, God sent his Son, born of a woman, born under the law, to redeem those under the law, that we might receive adoption to sonship.

~~~~~

In what ways have you not taken seriously the sacrifice of the eternal, all-powerful God coming as a baby to save humanity from sin? Thank Him for His humility, love, and goodness.

The Humility of God's Hunger

PSALM 50:12

> If I were hungry I would not tell you,
> for the world is mine, and all that is in it.

DEUTERONOMY 8:2–3

Remember how the LORD your God led you all the way in the wilderness these forty years, to humble and test you in order to know what was in your heart, whether or not you would keep his commands. He humbled you, causing you to hunger and then feeding you with manna, which neither you nor your ancestors had known, to teach you that man does not live on bread alone but on every word that comes from the mouth of the LORD.

LUKE 4:1–4

Jesus, full of the Holy Spirit, left the Jordan and was led by the Spirit into the wilderness, where for forty days he was tempted by the devil. He ate nothing during those days, and at the end of them he was hungry.

The devil said to him, "If you are the Son of God, tell this stone to become bread."

Jesus answered, "It is written: 'Man shall not live on bread alone.'"

Lord, you experienced more intense hunger during your temptation than I've ever known. I'm amazed that you, the Creator of all life, chose to experience such need. Thank you for your great humility.

The Humility of God's Rule

PSALM 45:3–4

> Gird your sword on your side, you mighty one;
>> clothe yourself with splendor and majesty.
> In your majesty ride forth victoriously
>> in the cause of truth, humility and justice;
>> let your right hand achieve awesome deeds.

ZECHARIAH 9:9

> Rejoice greatly, Daughter Zion!
>> Shout, Daughter Jerusalem!
> See, your king comes to you,
>> righteous and victorious,
> lowly and riding on a donkey,
>> on a colt, the foal of a donkey.

MATTHEW 11:28–30

Come to me, all you who are weary and burdened, and I will give you rest. Take my yoke upon you and learn from me, for I am gentle and humble in heart, and you will find rest for your souls. For my yoke is easy and my burden is light.

~~~~~

The King of all creation comes in lowly victory, inaugurating His kingdom of truth, justice, and righteousness with a humble heart.

The Humility of God's Suffering

PSALM 22:6–8

But I am a worm and not a man,
  scorned by everyone, despised by the people.
All who see me mock me;
  they hurl insults, shaking their heads.
"He trusts in the Lord," they say,
  "let the Lord rescue him.
Let him deliver him,
  since he delights in him."

ISAIAH 50:5–6

The Sovereign Lord has opened my ears;
  I have not been rebellious,
  I have not turned away.
I offered my back to those who beat me,
  my cheeks to those who pulled out my beard;
I did not hide my face
  from mocking and spitting.

MATTHEW 26:67–68

Then they spit in his face and struck him with their fists. Others slapped him and said, "Prophesy to us, Messiah. Who hit you?"

~~~~

What do you feel when you reflect on God's humble suffering on your behalf? Share your thoughts with Him, thanking Him for His goodness and sacrifice.

The Humility of God Becoming a Curse for Us

PSALM 109:26–28

> Help me, Lord my God;
>> save me according to your unfailing love.
> Let them know that it is your hand,
>> that you, Lord, have done it.
> While they curse, may you bless;
>> may those who attack me be put to shame,
>> but may your servant rejoice.

DEUTERONOMY 21:22–23

If someone guilty of a capital offense is put to death and their body is exposed on a pole, you must not leave the body hanging on the pole overnight. Be sure to bury it that same day, because anyone who is hung on a pole is under God's curse.

GALATIANS 3:13–14

Christ redeemed us from the curse of the law by becoming a curse for us, for it is written: "Cursed is everyone who is hung on a pole." He redeemed us in order that the blessing given to Abraham might come to the Gentiles through Christ Jesus, so that by faith we might receive the promise of the Spirit.

～～～

Lord, thank you for becoming a curse for me to redeem me from the curse of the law. When I forget, remind me of your incredible humility and unfailing love.

The Humility of God's Crucifixion

PSALM 22:17–19

> All my bones are on display;
> > people stare and gloat over me.
> They divide my clothes among them
> > and cast lots for my garment.

> But you, LORD, do not be far from me.
> > You are my strength; come quickly to help me.

ISAIAH 53:7–8

> He was oppressed and afflicted,
> > yet he did not open his mouth;
> he was led like a lamb to the slaughter,
> > and as a sheep before its shearers is silent,
> > so he did not open his mouth.
> By oppression and judgment he was taken away.
> > Yet who of his generation protested?
> For he was cut off from the land of the living;
> > for the transgression of my people he was punished.

MATTHEW 27:39–42

Those who passed by hurled insults at him, shaking their heads and saying, "You who are going to destroy the temple and build it in three days, save yourself! Come down from the cross, if you are the Son of God!" In the same way the chief priests, the teachers of the law and the elders mocked him. "He saved others," they said, "but he can't save himself!"

~~~~~

Jesus's crucifixion, the Creator's sacrificial death for His creation, was the ultimate act of humility.

The Good Works of Our Good God

PSALM 77:10–12

> Then I thought, "To this I will appeal:
>> the years when the Most High stretched out his right hand.
> I will remember the deeds of the LORD;
>> yes, I will remember your miracles of long ago.
> I will consider all your works
>> and meditate on all your mighty deeds."

GENESIS 1:31

God saw all that he had made, and it was very good. And there was evening, and there was morning—the sixth day.

ACTS 10:37–38

You know what has happened throughout the province of Judea, beginning in Galilee after the baptism that John preached—how God anointed Jesus of Nazareth with the Holy Spirit and power, and how he went around doing good and healing all who were under the power of the devil, because God was with him.

When have you doubted the goodness of what God is doing in your life? Talk openly with Him, asking Him to show you the goodness of His works.

God's Good Presence

PSALM 136:1

> Give thanks to the LORD, for he is good.
>> His love endures forever.

2 CHRONICLES 5:13–14

Accompanied by trumpets, cymbals and other instruments, the singers raised their voices in praise to the LORD and sang:

> "He is good;
>> his love endures forever."

Then the temple of the LORD was filled with the cloud, and the priests could not perform their service because of the cloud, for the glory of the LORD filled the temple of God.

HEBREWS 10:19–21

Therefore, brothers and sisters, . . . we have confidence to enter the Most Holy Place by the blood of Jesus, by a new and living way opened for us through the curtain, that is, his body, and . . . we have a great priest over the house of God.

~~~~~

Lord, your sacrifice has restored our relationship, and now I am always and eternally in your good presence. Please teach me to be aware of and grateful for your presence at all times.

DECEMBER

Love

What wondrous love is this, O my soul, O my soul!

What wondrous love is this, O my soul!

What wondrous love is this that caused the Lord
of bliss

to bear the dreadful curse for my soul, for my soul,

to bear the dreadful curse for my soul!

When I was sinking down, sinking down,
      sinking down,
when I was sinking down, sinking down,
when I was sinking down beneath God's
      righteous frown,
Christ laid aside His crown for my soul, for my soul,
Christ laid aside His crown for my soul.

To God and to the Lamb I will sing, I will sing;
to God and to the Lamb I will sing;
to God and to the Lamb, who is the great I AM.
While millions join the theme, I will sing, I will sing;
while millions join the theme, I will sing.

And when from death I'm free, I'll sing on,
      I'll sing on;
and when from death I'm free, I'll sing on.
And when from death I'm free, I'll sing His love
      for me,
and through eternity I'll sing on, I'll sing on,
and through eternity I'll sing on.

Author unknown, first published 1811

God Is Love

PSALM 118:1–4

> Give thanks to the LORD, for he is good;
>> his love endures forever.
>
> Let Israel say:
>> "His love endures forever."
> Let the house of Aaron say:
>> "His love endures forever."
> Let those who fear the LORD say:
>> "His love endures forever."

ZEPHANIAH 3:17

> The LORD your God is with you,
>> the Mighty Warrior who saves.
> He will take great delight in you;
>> in his love he will no longer rebuke you,
>> but will rejoice over you with singing.

1 JOHN 4:7–10

Dear friends, let us love one another, for love comes from God. Everyone who loves has been born of God and knows God. Whoever does not love does not know God, because God is love. This is how God showed his love among us: He sent his one and only Son into the world that we might live through him. This is love: not that we loved God, but that he loved us and sent his Son as an atoning sacrifice for our sins.

~~~~~~

God's love endures forever. He delights in you and sent His Son for you so you can love others too.

God's Unfailing Love

PSALM 33:20–22

We wait in hope for the Lord;
 he is our help and our shield.
In him our hearts rejoice,
 for we trust in his holy name.
May your unfailing love be with us, Lord,
 even as we put our hope in you.

HOSEA 3:1

The Lord said to me, "Go, show your love to your wife again, though she is loved by another man and is an adulteress. Love her as the Lord loves the Israelites, though they turn to other gods."

1 CORINTHIANS 13:6–8

Love does not delight in evil but rejoices with the truth. It always protects, always trusts, always hopes, always perseveres.

Love never fails.

~~~

How have you experienced Christlike love from another person in your life? Thank God that His love is unfailing: patient, kind, humble, selfless, slow to anger, and truthful.

God's Eternal Love

PSALM 52:8–9

> But I am like an olive tree
>   flourishing in the house of God;
> I trust in God's unfailing love
>   for ever and ever.
> For what you have done I will always praise you
>   in the presence of your faithful people.
> And I will hope in your name,
>   for your name is good.

JEREMIAH 33:10–11

"Yet in the towns of Judah and the streets of Jerusalem that are deserted, inhabited by neither people nor animals, there will be heard once more the sounds of joy and gladness, the voices of bride and bridegroom, and the voices of those who bring thank offerings to the house of the LORD, saying,

> 'Give thanks to the LORD Almighty,
>   for the LORD is good;
>   his love endures forever.'

For I will restore the fortunes of the land as they were before," says the LORD.

EPHESIANS 3:17–19

And I pray that you, being rooted and established in love, may have power, together with all the Lord's holy people, to grasp how wide and long and high and deep is the love of Christ, and to know this love that surpasses knowledge—that you may be filled to the measure of all the fullness of God.

~~~

Lord, your love is too wide and long and high and deep for me to comprehend. Thank you for loving me eternally and for rooting me in that love.

God Chooses Us in His Love

PSALM 13:3, 5–6

Look on me and answer, Lord my God.
 Give light to my eyes, or I will sleep in death. . . .

But I trust in your unfailing love;
 my heart rejoices in your salvation.
I will sing the Lord's praise,
 for he has been good to me.

DEUTERONOMY 10:14–15

To the Lord your God belong the heavens, even the highest heavens, the earth and everything in it. Yet the Lord set his affection on your ancestors and loved them, and he chose you, their descendants, above all the nations—as it is today.

JOHN 6:44–45

No one can come to me unless the Father who sent me draws them, and I will raise them up at the last day. It is written in the Prophets: "They will all be taught by God." Everyone who has heard the Father and learned from him comes to me.

~~~

God chose you in His unfailing love, and no one can take you from His hand.

God Forgives Us in His Love

PSALM 130:7–8

Israel, put your hope in the LORD,
    for with the LORD is unfailing love
    and with him is full redemption.
He himself will redeem Israel
    from all their sins.

PROVERBS 16:6–7

Through love and faithfulness sin is atoned for;
    through the fear of the LORD evil is avoided.

When the LORD takes pleasure in anyone's way,
    he causes their enemies to make peace with them.

2 CORINTHIANS 5:14–15

For Christ's love compels us, because we are convinced that one died for all, and therefore all died. And he died for all, that those who live should no longer live for themselves but for him who died for them and was raised again.

~~~~~~

Where are you living for yourself rather than for Christ? Confess to Him, and thank Him that He died so you can live in whole, loving relationships with Him, with others, and with yourself.

God Fills Us with His Love

PSALM 119:62–64

> At midnight I rise to give you thanks
> for your righteous laws.
> I am a friend to all who fear you,
> to all who follow your precepts.
> The earth is filled with your love, LORD;
> teach me your decrees.

PROVERBS 3:3–4

> Let love and faithfulness never leave you;
> bind them around your neck,
> write them on the tablet of your heart.
> Then you will win favor and a good name
> in the sight of God and man.

ROMANS 5:3–5

We also glory in our sufferings, because we know that suffering produces perseverance; perseverance, character; and character, hope. And hope does not put us to shame, because God's love has been poured out into our hearts through the Holy Spirit, who has been given to us.

~~~~~~

Lord, thank you for pouring your love into me through the power of your Holy Spirit. Write your love on my heart. Bind it around my neck. I want your love to overflow to everyone around me.

The Saving Love of Jesus

PSALM 6:4–5

Turn, Lᴏʀᴅ, and deliver me;
    save me because of your unfailing love.
Among the dead no one proclaims your name.
    Who praises you from the grave?

PROVERBS 10:11–12

The mouth of the righteous is a fountain of life,
    but the mouth of the wicked conceals violence.
Hatred stirs up conflict,
    but love covers over all wrongs.

JOHN 15:9–13

As the Father has loved me, so have I loved you. Now remain in my love. If you keep my commands, you will remain in my love, just as I have kept my Father's commands and remain in his love. I have told you this so that my joy may be in you and that your joy may be complete. My command is this: Love each other as I have loved you. Greater love has no one than this: to lay down one's life for one's friends.

~~~~~~

God loves you with the greatest love: He gave His life for you and invites you to remain forever in His love.

Our Triune God Is Relational

PSALM 107:8–9

> Let them give thanks to the LORD for his unfailing love
> and his wonderful deeds for mankind,
> for he satisfies the thirsty
> and fills the hungry with good things.

ISAIAH 6:6–8

Then one of the seraphim flew to me with a live coal in his hand, which he had taken with tongs from the altar. With it he touched my mouth and said, "See, this has touched your lips; your guilt is taken away and your sin atoned for."

Then I heard the voice of the LORD saying, "Whom shall I send? And who will go for us?"

LUKE 3:21–22

When all the people were being baptized, Jesus was baptized too. And as he was praying, heaven was opened and the Holy Spirit descended on him in bodily form like a dove. And a voice came from heaven: "You are my Son, whom I love; with you I am well pleased."

What word or phrase from the passages above stood out to you? Pause to talk with God about it.

Our God Pursues Relationship

PSALM 23:6

> Surely your goodness and love will follow me
>> all the days of my life,
> and I will dwell in the house of the Lord
>> forever.

GENESIS 3:8–9

Then the man and his wife heard the sound of the Lord God as he was walking in the garden in the cool of the day, and they hid from the Lord God among the trees of the garden. But the Lord God called to the man, "Where are you?"

LUKE 15:3–6

Then Jesus told them this parable: "Suppose one of you has a hundred sheep and loses one of them. Doesn't he leave the ninety-nine in the open country and go after the lost sheep until he finds it? And when he finds it, he joyfully puts it on his shoulders and goes home. Then he calls his friends and neighbors together and says, 'Rejoice with me; I have found my lost sheep.'"

~~~~~

Lord, too often I try to hide from you, ashamed of what I've done or what I've failed to do. Thank you for always pursuing me. Please help me to really know the joy you feel in finding me and having me.

Our God Makes Relationship Possible

PSALM 132:7–9

Let us go to his dwelling place,
　　let us worship at his footstool, saying,
"Arise, Lord, and come to your resting place,
　　you and the ark of your might.
May your priests be clothed with your righteousness."

ZECHARIAH 6:12–13

Tell him this is what the Lord Almighty says: "Here is the man whose name is the Branch, and he will branch out from his place and build the temple of the Lord. It is he who will build the temple of the Lord, and he will be clothed with majesty and will sit and rule on his throne. And he will be a priest on his throne. And there will be harmony between the two."

MATTHEW 27:50–51

And when Jesus had cried out again in a loud voice, he gave up his spirit.

At that moment the curtain of the temple was torn in two from top to bottom.

～～～

Through His death and resurrection, Jesus—the great High Priest— restored humanity's relationship with God.

Our God Knows Us Face to Face

PSALM 31:14–16

> But I trust in you, Lord;
>> I say, "You are my God."
> My times are in your hands;
>> deliver me from the hands of my enemies,
>> from those who pursue me.
> Let your face shine on your servant;
>> save me in your unfailing love.

EXODUS 33:9–11

As Moses went into the tent, the pillar of cloud would come down and stay at the entrance, while the Lord spoke with Moses. Whenever the people saw the pillar of cloud standing at the entrance to the tent, they all stood and worshiped, each at the entrance to their tent. The Lord would speak to Moses face to face, as one speaks to a friend.

1 CORINTHIANS 13:12

For now we see only a reflection as in a mirror; then we shall see face to face. Now I know in part; then I shall know fully, even as I am fully known.

~

In what ways do you think you see God unclearly or inaccurately? Ask Him to show himself to you, and to give you patience until you fully know Him.

Christ Our Brother

PSALM 22:22–24

> I will declare your name to my people;
> in the assembly I will praise you.
> You who fear the LORD, praise him!
> All you descendants of Jacob, honor him!
> Revere him, all you descendants of Israel!
> For he has not despised or scorned
> the suffering of the afflicted one;
> he has not hidden his face from him
> but has listened to his cry for help.

PROVERBS 18:24

> One who has unreliable friends soon comes to ruin,
> but there is a friend who sticks closer than a brother.

HEBREWS 2:11–12

Both the one who makes people holy and those who are made holy are of the same family. So Jesus is not ashamed to call them brothers and sisters. He says,

> "I will declare your name to my brothers and sisters;
> in the assembly I will sing your praises."

~

Lord, thank you for making us family in Jesus, and for calling me your sibling. I'm so grateful that you are making me holy as you are holy.

Our Mothering God

PSALM 131:2–3

> But I have calmed and quieted myself,
>> I am like a weaned child with its mother;
>> like a weaned child I am content.
>
> Israel, put your hope in the LORD
>> both now and forevermore.

ISAIAH 66:12–13

> For this is what the LORD says:
>
> "I will extend peace to her like a river,
>> and the wealth of nations like a flooding stream;
> you will nurse and be carried on her arm
>> and dandled on her knees.
> As a mother comforts her child,
>> so will I comfort you;
>> and you will be comforted over Jerusalem."

LUKE 13:34

> Jerusalem, Jerusalem, you who kill the prophets and stone those sent to you, how often I have longed to gather your children together, as a hen gathers her chicks under her wings, and you were not willing.

God is a nurturing parent who provides for you, carries you, comforts you, and guides you.

God Our Husband

PSALM 42:8

> By day the LORD directs his love,
>   at night his song is with me—
>   a prayer to the God of my life.

HOSEA 2:16

> "In that day," declares the LORD,
>   "you will call me 'my husband';
>   you will no longer call me 'my master.'"

REVELATION 21:2–4

I saw the Holy City, the new Jerusalem, coming down out of heaven from God, prepared as a bride beautifully dressed for her husband. And I heard a loud voice from the throne saying, "Look! God's dwelling place is now among the people, and he will dwell with them. They will be his people, and God himself will be with them and be their God. 'He will wipe every tear from their eyes. There will be no more death' or mourning or crying or pain, for the old order of things has passed away."

~~~

What does sharing a loving, intimate, covenantal relationship with God mean to you? Talk with Him about it, and thank Him for being yours.

The Lord Is Near

PSALM 34:17–18

The righteous cry out, and the LORD hears them;
 he delivers them from all their troubles.
The LORD is close to the brokenhearted
 and saves those who are crushed in spirit.

ISAIAH 41:9–10

I took you from the ends of the earth,
 from its farthest corners I called you.
I said, "You are my servant";
 I have chosen you and have not rejected you.
So do not fear, for I am with you;
 do not be dismayed, for I am your God.
I will strengthen you and help you;
 I will uphold you with my righteous right hand.

PHILIPPIANS 4:4–7

Rejoice in the Lord always. I will say it again: Rejoice! Let your gentleness be evident to all. The Lord is near. Do not be anxious about anything, but in every situation, by prayer and petition, with thanksgiving, present your requests to God. And the peace of God, which transcends all understanding, will guard your hearts and your minds in Christ Jesus.

Lord, in every corner of creation, you are near. Thank you for hearing my voice whenever I call. I want your peace, strength, and joy near me too.

God's Glorious Nearness

PSALM 68:32–35

Sing to God, you kingdoms of the earth,
  sing praise to the Lord,
to him who rides across the highest heavens, the ancient heavens,
  who thunders with mighty voice.
Proclaim the power of God,
  whose majesty is over Israel,
  whose power is in the heavens.
You, God, are awesome in your sanctuary;
  the God of Israel gives power and strength to his people.

EXODUS 24:9–11

Moses and Aaron, Nadab and Abihu, and the seventy elders of Israel
went up and saw the God of Israel. Under his feet was something like a
pavement made of lapis lazuli, as bright blue as the sky. But God did not
raise his hand against these leaders of the Israelites; they saw God, and
they ate and drank.

REVELATION 4:2–5

At once I was in the Spirit, and there before me was a throne in
heaven with someone sitting on it. And the one who sat there had the
appearance of jasper and ruby. A rainbow that shone like an emerald
encircled the throne. Surrounding the throne were twenty-four other
thrones, and seated on them were twenty-four elders. . . . From the
throne came flashes of lightning, rumblings and peals of thunder.

*God comes near in His transcendent glory so you can live and worship
in His presence.*

God Draws Near to Those
Who Draw Near to Him

PSALM 34:15–16

> The eyes of the LORD are on the righteous,
>> and his ears are attentive to their cry;
> but the face of the LORD is against those who do evil.

2 CHRONICLES 15:2–4

The LORD is with you when you are with him. If you seek him, he will be found by you, but if you forsake him, he will forsake you. For a long time Israel was without the true God, without a priest to teach and without the law. But in their distress they turned to the LORD, the God of Israel, and sought him, and he was found by them.

JAMES 4:7–10

Submit yourselves, then, to God. Resist the devil, and he will flee from you. Come near to God and he will come near to you. Wash your hands, you sinners, and purify your hearts, you double-minded. Grieve, mourn and wail. Change your laughter to mourning and your joy to gloom. Humble yourselves before the Lord, and he will lift you up.

~~~

Where have you been turning away from God? Confess to Him, and grieve that you have been choosing distance from Him. Tell Him that you want to humble yourself and purify your heart.

God Is Near Those He Forgives

PSALM 105:2–4

Sing to him, sing praise to him;
　　tell of all his wonderful acts.
Glory in his holy name;
　　let the hearts of those who seek the LORD rejoice.
Look to the LORD and his strength;
　　seek his face always.

ISAIAH 50:8–9

He who vindicates me is near.
　　Who then will bring charges against me?
　　Let us face each other!
Who is my accuser?
　　Let him confront me!
It is the Sovereign LORD who helps me.
　　Who will condemn me?

ACTS 2:38–39

Peter replied, "Repent and be baptized, every one of you, in the name of Jesus Christ for the forgiveness of your sins. And you will receive the gift of the Holy Spirit. The promise is for you and your children and for all who are far off—for all whom the Lord our God will call."

~~~~~~

Lord, thank you for forgiving me. When I was far off, you called me in your love and came near. Your strength and faithful promise bring me such joy.

God Is Near His Chosen People

PSALM 84:8–10

Hear my prayer, Lord God Almighty;
    listen to me, God of Jacob.
Look on our shield, O God;
    look with favor on your anointed one.

Better is one day in your courts
    than a thousand elsewhere;
I would rather be a doorkeeper in the house of my God
    than dwell in the tents of the wicked.

DEUTERONOMY 31:7–8

Then Moses summoned Joshua and said to him in the presence of all Israel, "Be strong and courageous, for you must go with this people into the land that the Lord swore to their ancestors to give them, and you must divide it among them as their inheritance. The Lord himself goes before you and will be with you; he will never leave you nor forsake you. Do not be afraid; do not be discouraged."

JOHN 14:18–20

I will not leave you as orphans; I will come to you. Before long, the world will not see me anymore, but you will see me. Because I live, you also will live. On that day you will realize that I am in my Father, and you are in me, and I am in you.

～～

God never leaves nor forsakes His people. You are in Him, and He is in you.

God Is Near All People

PSALM 65:2–3

You who answer prayer,
    to you all people will come.
When we were overwhelmed by sins,
    you forgave our transgressions.

ISAIAH 52:9–10

Burst into songs of joy together,
    you ruins of Jerusalem,
for the LORD has comforted his people,
    he has redeemed Jerusalem.
The LORD will lay bare his holy arm
    in the sight of all the nations,
and all the ends of the earth will see
    the salvation of our God.

JOHN 12:30–33

Jesus said, "This voice was for your benefit, not mine. Now is the time for judgment on this world; now the prince of this world will be driven out. And I, when I am lifted up from the earth, will draw all people to myself." He said this to show the kind of death he was going to die.

~~~~~

When have you seen God near those who don't yet know Him? Thank Him that He is making His salvation known to the ends of the earth, and ask Him to give you His heart for others.

God Makes His Home among Us

PSALM 91:1–2, 4

Whoever dwells in the shelter of the Most High
    will rest in the shadow of the Almighty.
I will say of the LORD, "He is my refuge and my fortress,
    my God, in whom I trust." . . .

He will cover you with his feathers,
    and under his wings you will find refuge;
    his faithfulness will be your shield and rampart.

EZEKIEL 48:34–35

On the west side, which is 4,500 cubits long, will be three gates: the gate of Gad, the gate of Asher and the gate of Naphtali.

The distance all around will be 18,000 cubits.

And the name of the city from that time on will be:

THE LORD IS THERE.

REVELATION 22:3–5

The throne of God and of the Lamb will be in the city, and his servants will serve him. They will see his face, and his name will be on their foreheads. There will be no more night. They will not need the light of a lamp or the light of the sun, for the Lord God will give them light. And they will reign for ever and ever.

~~~~~

Lord, you are making your home with me, so I can rest under your wings and live forever in your light. Teach me to live every day knowing you are near.

God Is Incarnate

PSALM 46:11

The LORD Almighty is with us;
    the God of Jacob is our fortress.

ISAIAH 9:1–2

In the past he humbled the land of Zebulun and the land of
Naphtali, but in the future he will honor Galilee of the nations, by the
Way of the Sea, beyond the Jordan—

The people walking in darkness
    have seen a great light;
on those living in the land of deep darkness
    a light has dawned.

MATTHEW 1:20–23

"Joseph son of David, do not be afraid to take Mary home as your
wife, because what is conceived in her is from the Holy Spirit. She will
give birth to a son, and you are to give him the name Jesus, because he
will save his people from their sins."

All this took place to fulfill what the Lord had said through the
prophet: "The virgin will conceive and give birth to a son, and they will
call him Immanuel" (which means "God with us").

*In His love for His creation, God became human to save humanity
from their sins.*

Jesus, the God-Man

PSALM 40:6–8

Sacrifice and offering you did not desire—
   but my ears you have opened—
   burnt offerings and sin offerings you did not require.
Then I said, "Here I am, I have come—
   it is written about me in the scroll.
I desire to do your will, my God;
   your law is within my heart." *

GENESIS 3:14–15

So the Lord God said to the serpent, "Because you have done this, . . .

"I will put enmity
   between you and the woman,
   and between your offspring and hers;
he will crush your head,
   and you will strike his heel."

HEBREWS 2:14–15

Since the children have flesh and blood, [Jesus] too shared in their humanity so that by his death he might break the power of him who holds the power of death—that is, the devil—and free those who all their lives were held in slavery by their fear of death.

~~~~~

Does the fear of death have a hold over you? Share your fears with Jesus, and thank Him that as both God and man, He was able to break the power of death over humankind.

---

* Many Old Testament prophecies found their fulfillment in Jesus's life and ministry. Jesus himself called attention to this fact in Luke 4:14–21.

Jesus, Our Sure Foundation

PSALM 118:21–23

> I will give you thanks, for you answered me;
>> you have become my salvation.
>
> The stone the builders rejected
>> has become the cornerstone;
> the LORD has done this,
>> and it is marvelous in our eyes.

ISAIAH 28:16–17

> See, I lay a stone in Zion, a tested stone,
>> a precious cornerstone for a sure foundation;
> the one who relies on it
>> will never be stricken with panic.
> I will make justice the measuring line
>> and righteousness the plumb line.

MATTHEW 21:42–44

> Jesus said to them, "Have you never read in the Scriptures:
>
> "'The stone the builders rejected
>> has become the cornerstone . . .'?
>
> "Therefore I tell you that the kingdom of God will be taken away from you and given to a people who will produce its fruit. Anyone who falls on this stone will be broken to pieces; anyone on whom it falls will be crushed."

Lord, thank you for founding your kingdom of righteousness on the life, death, and resurrection of Jesus. Please produce your kingdom fruit in me.

Jesus, the Son of David

PSALM 72:1–2

Endow the king with your justice, O God,
  the royal son with your righteousness.
May he judge your people in righteousness,
  your afflicted ones with justice.

2 SAMUEL 7:15–17

"But my love will never be taken away from him, as I took it away from Saul, whom I removed from before you. Your house and your kingdom will endure forever before me; your throne will be established forever."

Nathan reported to David all the words of this entire revelation.

LUKE 1:30–33

But the angel said to her, "Do not be afraid, Mary; you have found favor with God. You will conceive and give birth to a son, and you are to call him Jesus. He will be great and will be called the Son of the Most High. The Lord God will give him the throne of his father David, and he will reign over Jacob's descendants forever; his kingdom will never end."

Jesus was born into David's royal line to establish His kingdom on the earth and to fulfill God's promise to bring His blessing to all nations through the people of Israel.

Jesus, Our Healing

PSALM 30:1–3

I will exalt you, LORD,
>for you lifted me out of the depths
>and did not let my enemies gloat over me.
LORD my God, I called to you for help,
>and you healed me.
You, LORD, brought me up from the realm of the dead;
>you spared me from going down to the pit.

NUMBERS 21:8–9

The LORD said to Moses, "Make a snake and put it up on a pole; anyone who is bitten can look at it and live." So Moses made a bronze snake and put it up on a pole. Then when anyone was bitten by a snake and looked at the bronze snake, they lived.

JOHN 3:13–15

No one has ever gone into heaven except the one who came from heaven—the Son of Man. Just as Moses lifted up the snake in the wilderness, so the Son of Man must be lifted up, that everyone who believes may have eternal life in him.

~~~~~

How have you experienced Jesus's healing—relational, emotional, or physical—in your life? Praise Him that He came to bring eternal life to all who turn and look to Him.

Jesus, the God-Man
Who Tasted Death for Humanity

PSALM 22:14–15

I am poured out like water,
and all my bones are out of joint.
My heart has turned to wax;
it has melted within me. . . .
you lay me in the dust of death.

ISAIAH 53:9, 12

He was assigned a grave with the wicked,
and with the rich in his death,
though he had done no violence,
nor was any deceit in his mouth. . . .

Therefore I will give him a portion among the great,
and he will divide the spoils with the strong,
because he poured out his life unto death,
and was numbered with the transgressors.
For he bore the sin of many,
and made intercession for the transgressors.

ROMANS 8:3–4

For what the law was powerless to do because it was weakened by
the flesh, God did by sending his own Son in the likeness of sinful flesh
to be a sin offering. And so he condemned sin in the flesh, in order that
the righteous requirement of the law might be fully met in us, who do
not live according to the flesh but according to the Spirit.

~~~~~

*Lord, you became human and poured out your life unto death to bear
my sins in your body. Thank you for loving me so much and giving
me your Spirit.*

Jesus, the God-Man
Who Brings New Life

PSALM 111:9

> He provided redemption for his people;
>> he ordained his covenant forever—
>> holy and awesome is his name.

JOB 14:14–16

> If someone dies, will they live again?
>> All the days of my hard service
>> I will wait for my renewal to come.
> You will call and I will answer you;
>> you will long for the creature your hands have made.
> Surely then you will count my steps
>> but not keep track of my sin.

ROMANS 5:18–19

Consequently, just as one trespass resulted in condemnation for all people, so also one righteous act resulted in justification and life for all people. For just as through the disobedience of the one man the many were made sinners, so also through the obedience of the one man the many will be made righteous.

~~~~~~

Jesus lived, died, and rose again to give you new life, legally acquit your sins, and right your relationships with Him and with others.

The Wonders of God's Love

PSALM 17:6–8

I call on you, my God, for you will answer me;
   turn your ear to me and hear my prayer.
Show me the wonders of your great love,
   you who save by your right hand
      those who take refuge in you from their foes.
Keep me as the apple of your eye;
   hide me in the shadow of your wings.

ISAIAH 65:1–2

I revealed myself to those who did not ask for me;
   I was found by those who did not seek me.
To a nation that did not call on my name,
   I said, "Here am I, here am I."
All day long I have held out my hands
   to an obstinate people,
who walk in ways not good,
   pursuing their own imaginations.

1 JOHN 4:16–18

God is love. Whoever lives in love lives in God, and God in them. This is how love is made complete among us so that we will have confidence on the day of judgment: In this world we are like Jesus. There is no fear in love. But perfect love drives out fear.

*Where have you obstinately ignored God's presence and love?
Talk with Him about it, thanking Him that He reveals himself even
when you aren't seeking Him. Ask Him to help you live in His love.*

God's Inseparable Love

PSALM 44:22–23

> Yet for your sake we face death all day long;
>> we are considered as sheep to be slaughtered.
>
> Awake, Lord! Why do you sleep?
>> Rouse yourself! Do not reject us forever.

ISAIAH 43:4–6

> Since you are precious and honored in my sight,
>> and because I love you,
> I will give people in exchange for you,
>> nations in exchange for your life.
> Do not be afraid, for I am with you;
>> I will bring your children from the east
>> and gather you from the west. . . .
> Bring my sons from afar
>> and my daughters from the ends of the earth.

ROMANS 8:35–37

Who shall separate us from the love of Christ? Shall trouble or hardship or persecution or famine or nakedness or danger or sword? As it is written:

> "For your sake we face death all day long;
>> we are considered as sheep to be slaughtered."

No, in all these things we are more than conquerors through him who loved us.

~~~~~

Lord, thank you that nothing in all creation can separate me from your love. You are always attentive to me, and I am precious in your sight.

God's Love Is Making Us New

PSALM 96:1–3

Sing to the LORD a new song;
    sing to the LORD, all the earth.
Sing to the LORD, praise his name;
    proclaim his salvation day after day.
Declare his glory among the nations,
    his marvelous deeds among all peoples.

ISAIAH 65:17–18

See, I will create
    new heavens and a new earth.
The former things will not be remembered,
    nor will they come to mind.
But be glad and rejoice forever
    in what I will create.

2 CORINTHIANS 5:17–19

Therefore, if anyone is in Christ, the new creation has come: The old has gone, the new is here! All this is from God, who reconciled us to himself through Christ and gave us the ministry of reconciliation: that God was reconciling the world to himself in Christ, not counting people's sins against them. And he has committed to us the message of reconciliation.

~~~~~~~~~

God is making a new creation, reconciling the world to himself through the love of Christ.